YOUR BEST DAYS
are ahead of YOU

SHANE KEMPTON

YOUR BEST DAYS
are ahead of YOU

Reverse the rut and unleash
the best version of you

© Shane Kempton 2019

The moral right of the author has been asserted.

All rights reserved. Except as permitted under the *Australian Copyright Act 1968*, no part of this book may be reproduced or transmitted by any person or entity, in any form or by any means, electronic or mechanical, including photocopying, recording, scanning or by any information storage and retrieval system, without prior permission in writing from the author.

Cover Design by Ellie Schroeder – ellieschroeder.com
Typeset in 12/16 pt Bembo by Post Pre-press Group, Brisbane
PO Box 1638, Carindale, Queensland 4152 Australia

Cataloguing-in-Publication data is available from the National Library of Australia

ISBN: 978-0-6487398-0-7 (pbk)
ISBN: 978-0-6487398-2-1 (ePub)
ISBN: 978-0-6487398-1-4 (mobi)

I dedicate this book to family.
You don't have to share the same blood to be family.
The people who stand by you, through thick and thin,
in the sunshine and the storms, without flinching
and steadfast, they are your family.

Brothers and Sisters

Thank you

Shane Kempton

Contents

Introduction	1

PART 1: THE STORIES

Chapter 1:	DISCOVER YOUR PATCH	13
Chapter 2:	YOUR COMPELLING VISION	23
Chapter 3:	FROM WORRIER TO WARRIOR	37
Chapter 4:	BECOMING THE CAUSE	48
Chapter 5:	FOCUSED GAME PLAN	59
Chapter 6:	THE HOME TEAM ADVANTAGE	68

PART II: THE LESSONS

Chapter 7:	THE POWER OF FUTURE PACING	79
Chapter 8:	MY SUCCESS TRINITY	93
Chapter 9:	THE MASTER LIFE MODEL	105
Chapter 10:	THE BEST VERSION OF YOU BLUEPRINT	121
Chapter 11:	SETTING UP YOUR WINNING ROUTINES	132
Chapter 12:	GRATITUDE 2.0 AND MEDITATION	142
Chapter 13:	BECOMING THE ROUTINE WARRIOR	152
Chapter 14:	YOUR BEST DAYS ARE AHEAD OF YOU	163

Conclusion	170
So, what's next?	173
About Shane Kempton	179

INTRODUCTION

It's 4:30am on the 4th of November. A young single mother is in labour.

She's terrified of the thought of giving birth. She's terrified that the baby she's carried for nine months will be taken away from her against her will and adopted out. How could this happen again? And this is not the first time.

Four years earlier, the same situation was unfolding.

This same young teenage girl was working at her first job in a male-dominated industry, innocent to the world of money and power. An older, married employer took advantage of her and she fell pregnant.

In the 60s, teenage pregnancy was pretty taboo. So, her parents flew their teenage girl to another Australian State to give birth to a child that would be immediately adopted out to another family.

Four years later, that same young lady in her early 20s was about to go through the same harrowing experience once again.

Yet this time, things were a bit different. She had a boyfriend and he was the father of this child.

Once again, her parents thought she was too young to have a child. They were afraid her pregnancy would bring shame to the family. Her boyfriend asked her to run away with him, but they put a stop to that too.

With her labour pains intensifying as her parents ushered her to the car to take her to hospital, she was about to re-live the heart-breaking process of losing another child to the system.

But this time, her siblings stepped in.

Her older brother, younger sister and younger brother pleaded with their parents not to put her through this awful experience again. They promised to help raise the child and begged them not to take the baby away.

After hours of yelling, arguing, tears and pleading, they made the decision she could keep the baby.

Around 8:00am on the 4th November 1969, this young woman, my mother gave birth to me.

As promised, I was raised by my mother, her brothers and sister and my grandparents.

I will always be grateful to my mother, my aunty and two uncles for fighting for me.

For giving me the chance to be with my family and to grow up with their warmth and love around me.

Four decades later, we were even reunited with my half-brother Andy and he is a part of our family once again.

Mum and I lived with my grandparents until I started high school and my grandparents provided me with love and support as best they could. Pop, a World War II veteran, was my father figure and Nan was the strong matriarch of the family who ruled the roost.

Both Mum and Nan were cooks, so much of my early life was

spent growing up around the hotels where they prepared meals for the clientele, while Pop was an orderly at the local hospital.

Life was tough. We never had a lot of money and we struggled to pay the bills each month, but I had a pretty happy childhood despite the financial rut.

My story might be different to yours, but it is also has a common theme.

Starting out life in a generational rut or feeling like you're on the back foot is a universal experience and it has provided me with the motivation to try and live a better life.

If you're reading this book, there's a good chance you've felt stuck in the past, you're stuck now or you want to change something in your life.

Or you might be feeling flat and unmotivated because you think your best days are behind you and you've had enough of feeling this way.

Good! You've got the right book in your hands.

This book is a practical guide to shift your attention from the good old days of the past, to believing and knowing your best days are ahead of you.

To do that, we have to help you free up your attention, mindset and beliefs about what's possible.

There are many terms for feeling stuck but the most common is a being in a *rut*. An actual rut is a deep groove in the ground, typically caused by an animal, bike or car. If you step in it, you can literally get *stuck*.

When it comes to our emotional lives, a rut is often the boring or crippling routine of our thoughts, habits or lifestyle that can be hard to break, leaving you feeling stuck.

Most people find themselves in a rut, or say they feel their life is like *Groundhog Day*, repeating the same old stuff, day in, day out.

Simply put, if you're stuck in a rut, you've been doing the same old thing for too long. You feel like you've got nothing to look forward to and you're left reminiscing about the good old days of the past.

We often spend most of our waking hours at work, so it's common to find your job boring or uninspiring. You might try changing but nothing seems to pull you out of the rut.

Many of us also find ourselves in a personal, professional, relationship, career, wealth, health or even a success rut.

The mundane reality of the 9 to 5 routine.

Partying too hard on the weekend and starting all over again on Monday morning with watery, red eyes and hangover guilt.

Pay day arrives and after forking out money for rent or mortgage and bills, there's barely any left. So, you spend the weekend watching Netflix and scrolling mindlessly though Facebook and saying no to party invites.

You could have it all but you just feel empty. The fanciest car, the coolest holiday and the latest labels just don't seem to fill the void inside of you.

You've tried every fad diet, gruelling exercise routine and fasting cleanse known to mankind, but you still can't lose that stubborn weight that's been hanging onto your hips and thighs for years.

Maybe you're attending VIP seminars, workshops and conferences. Doing all the training. Reading all the recommended books and yet, somehow, success eludes you.

And there always seems to be more 'month' than money.

Even businesses and teams can be in a collective rut, that is, like a herd of animals, they just go on following each other, repeating the same old actions, dealing with the same old clients and yet they expect new results.

That was me.

During my 50 years on this planet, I've experienced every possible rut life could throw at me. Which is why I know first-hand how soul-depleting it is.

Being in a rut is disempowering and comes with feelings of helplessness, aimlessness and despair.

Worse yet, the more we continue with the boring routines that created the rut, the deeper it gets and the more stuck we feel.

Believe me, I know. I've been a prisoner in the past to the ruts I've caused in my life. Those ruts have occurred at the bottom of the mountain, during the climb and at the peak.

And I know I'm not the only one. Most of my clients have come to me with similar challenges.

And ruts don't discriminate.

They don't care how old you are. How much money you have. How fit and strong you are. What career or profession you're in. Whether you're a start-up entrepreneur or seasoned business owner or stay-at-home parent.

Nope. Ruts can happen to anyone and when you find yourself in one, you feel vulnerable. Ruts bring you down and leave you feeling at your lowest.

No matter how much willpower you use in an attempt to stay positive, the positivity passes and you feel like crap because you just can't sustain this 'fake' state of being.

And nothing you do seems to work.

My ruts have kept me searching for happiness and fulfilment in all sorts of places.

The good news is this: there's a set of skills, a Master Life Model and a Blueprint that will help you avoid the slippery slopes and deep trenches of a rut. A set of principles that will get you believing and knowing that your best days are definitely ahead of you.

Even better, this Model and Blueprint comes with a bonus side effect: **it's also a secret map to becoming the best version of you.**

When you apply the techniques, tactics and routines shared in this book, you're on the path to becoming the best version of yourself and you naturally create the conditions that are polar opposite to being in a rut.

You find yourself standing on the top of a mountain, with a clear vision and a sense of possibility. You switch from survive to thrive. You get creative and bold. You shift from existing to *living*.

You can't reverse the rut by doing the same things over and over again that got you there.

This book will help you stop and to take stock of your life. You'll reflect on every decision you've made in order to assess which beliefs are serving you and which ones are not.

The aim is then to 'future pace' a more desirable reality, reverse-engineer it and harness the power of new skills, habits and routines to make better choices that serve you.

This process will remind you that what you did before may not have been the best path and it didn't deliver the outcomes or lifestyle you imagined. It will also help you avoid defaulting back to those old, non-serving habits.

Want to know the truth about this process? It's simple but it's not easy.

There will be times you'll want to stay in your familiar, yet not so comfortable comfort zone. In those times, it's critical to remember these are also the main causes of your rut. They're why you feel stuck to begin with.

So, here's my call to action for you.

It's time to do the work, rise above the rut and experience the life you desire.

The **Master Life Model** and **Best Version of You (BVOY) Blueprint** that I developed were born out of my mission to get out of the rut of an ordinary existence and find my unique meaning and purpose in life.

And I want to do the same for *you*.

My three-decade obsession with self-development (which continues to this day) has created a very unique blend of life experiences:

- Small business and corporate success
- Time in the military, working alongside Special Forces Soldiers
- Membership in some of the world's most secretive societies
- Playing and coaching elite sports teams
- Hanging out in the dark world of motorcycle gangs
- Studying many of the world's religions and walking the paths of mystical and spiritual ways
- Charity work including assisting our modern-day military veterans, and
- Promoting good men's mental health.

My life's journey, with all its ups and downs, successes and failures has placed me in a very unique situation. It's gifted me with the foresight and ability to dissect the above experiences and find the **golden thread of success** that weaves itself around all of them.

This is a book of discovery, stories, laughs, tears, knowledge, success and failures.

It will take you on a journey into many different worlds and experiences.

Into the shadows and into the light, from the boardroom to the clubhouse, from the office to the temple, from the latest modern day medical and scientific discoveries to 2500-year old wisdom.

From the outer world to the inner world.

I've condensed decades of wisdom and practical experience into a set of powerful and easy to implement tactics and routines to help you realise that your best days are most certainly ahead of you, wherever you may be in your life right now.

I am committed to helping you find the path to the **best version of you**.

That's why I created my **Master Life Model** incorporating the five key building blocks you need to reverse the rut and the **Best Version of You Blueprint** to help you map out and live your best life.

As you read this book, don't get hung up on my journey or the non-traditional paths I've followed. This book's not going to ask you to believe in anything you can't prove or that's just a theory.

Everything in this book has come from real life experiences, replicated with my coaching clients. Most importantly, if you follow the pragmatic, step-by-step instructions in this book, you can apply my Model and Blueprint to your life.

This is a practical, powerful and proven guide and not a work of fiction or theory for you to try. *But you do have to do the work.* Just reading this book is not going to change your life unless *you* change your life.

It's not a get rich quick scheme. But it is a more efficient way to find peace, happiness, health, success and fulfilment in your life.

I've written the book in two parts.

Part 1 is made up of my life experiences, shared with you via some very funny (and sometimes not so funny) stories. They will entertain and educate you.

Part 2 packages up those stories into a series of lessons, coaching models, tactics and routines you can implement into your life.

If you want to skip the back stories and get stuck into the learning, feel free to start reading from Part 2. If you want to know the source of the learning, start from Part 1. It's your book, your experience, your choice.

There are links to bonus and exclusive downloads throughout the book and the opportunity to leave comments, which I encourage you to do.

And finally, if there's one thing you need to believe that will provide the foundation for you to begin your climb out of your rut and towards your mountain top, it's this:

Your best days are ahead of you.

Here's to unleashing the best version of you.

Enjoy the journey.

Shane Kempton

PART 1

THE STORIES

CHAPTER 1: DISCOVER YOUR PATCH

I was standing back to back with my best mate Kev, behind the fortified walls of a one percenter's (1%) motorcycle gang's clubhouse.

Ten bikies formed a circle around us in the dimly lit carpark.

Now, I'm a pretty hefty guy. 193cm and (back then) a solid 110kg. My mates used to call me Big Rig.

But these guys made me look like David staring up at an army of Goliaths. All I could see were 6-foot plus men soaring above me, staring down.

Steroid-enhanced muscles bulging and twitching in their tight black t-shirts and sleeveless, leather jackets. They are tattooed from top to bottom. Their faces mean, their intentions even worse.

These guys were the real deal. No movie star "Sons of Anarchy" wannabes. These guys were the authentic "1% ers" people talk about in hushed voices.

I swallowed hard and tried to muster up a non-threatening, nervous smile, but there was no response.

Only emotionless stares as they formed a tight circle around Kev and I, advancing upon us with an air of intimidation.

Earlier that day, we'd received a call from the Club President, demanding that we meet at the clubhouse at 7:00 pm sharp, with strict instructions not to be late if we wanted our request to be heard.

We'd arrived right on time, greeted by a gruff club member, gazing through a peephole in a 10-foot tall steel gate.

"What do you two bastards want?" he grunted.

After we identified ourselves, we heard several locks click and the gates swung open. They ushered us into an empty room and told us to leave our phones in a metal box.

Next, they quietly led us out to that carpark and told us not to move until the Club President and the rest of the Committee arrived.

Without looking too obvious, I surveyed my surroundings.

The main building was a large industrial unit, with a couple of locked buildings separate to the main unit that looked like garages or workshops. I could see at least 100 proud Harley Davidsons parked around the lot and several big black vans.

Kev and I just stood there in anxious anticipation for at least 15 minutes, but it felt like a lifetime.

A million thoughts and questions were rushing through my head.

How many people are in there?
Why did they take our phones?
Who knows we're here?
Have they mistaken us for some rival gang?
Will I be leaving here on my bike, in a cab? Or in an ambulance?

There we were, in a dark carpark locked away from the world, behind the massive gates of a genuine "1%" motorcycle gang clubhouse, with no phone and no idea what was about to happen.

That's when 10 of the most intimidating club members approached us with their President and formed a circle around us. The thought that *no one in the world knew we were there* sent a shiver down my spine.

That's how we found ourselves here, in this carpark, surrounded by ten menacing men, staring at us like predators stalking their prey, waiting to hear my response to the question just asked by their President.

There was an awkward silence. I felt my pulse quicken, a bead of sweat formed on my brow.

I steadied my feet in anticipation of what would inevitably happen next.

That's when I felt Kev press his back hard against mine.

Kev turned his head slightly sideways and whispered in my ear:

"Don't worry, brother. No matter what, I've got your back."
"I believe in what we are doing. We're ready for this".

And that's when I knew I'd found my *patch*.

You see, motorcycle club members are often seen wearing leather vests or jackets adorned with colourful and vibrant patches and emblems.

These patches and emblems aren't just there for decoration. They have meanings and symbolism and hidden information only known to bikers.

You use these patches to identify a biker's club, position, length of membership, and any other achievements they may have earned.

They also represent what you're all about and what tribe you belong to.

Kev and I were there for a reason. And I'm guessing you're wondering what that reason was. What we wanted to ask the Club President and why we were there at all.

Well, *patches* are the reason. You see, Kev and I were there to ask the Club President permission to have our own 'patch.' A motorcycle club of our own.

We had a **shared vision and mission** and we had each other's back, no matter what his response was. Let me explain.

My Pop rode motorcycles in the military. Later on, motorcycles became a personal love of mine too.

When he returned from active service, like many veterans, he found himself in a rut, struggling to settle back into civilian life.

Like many veterans, he turned to alcohol to numb the atrocities he'd witnessed during the war and this only accelerated the spiral downwards.

Back then, PTSD wasn't a thing and you were told to harden up and get on with life.

Fast forward to 2013, after five years of fulltime military service (1995 to 2000) and some years in the Army Reserves, I wanted to do something to help the modern-day veterans adapt to life back home.

My passion to help those returning servicemen and women who were struggling with PTSD, or just re-establishing themselves back into civilian life had become my mission.

Because I know and have seen just how hard that adjustment is. Just imagine a highly trained soldier who's been on active duty, working and training in the toughest of environments, alongside other soldiers.

You know they have your back, and you have theirs. You are 100% focused on a common cause and mission you believe in and you put your life on the line to achieve it every single day without question.

It's a high adrenalin environment, so far removed from the ordinary civilian life we're accustomed too. When these soldiers (airmen and seamen) leave the service, some find their skills may not be required in civilian life.

They go from feeling a great sense of purpose to asking themselves: *Where do I belong?*

Some look for ways to escape or to numb the pain, by isolating themselves or masking their symptoms with drugs or alcohol. This deepens the rut they've found themselves in.

Having seen military friends and family suffer like this after the service they provided to our country, I wanted to do something about it.

I had a newfound vision and mission.

I decided to combine my love of motorcycles and the freedom of the open road, with the structure and feel of the military and set up a motorcycle club for veterans and those who supported them.

My vision was to have a club where our returning soldiers had a haven, a sense of belonging and purpose through serving again.

Where they could help other veterans (especially older ones) by visiting them at their homes, at the RSLs and generally helping to take the focus off themselves and their thoughts.

The ride on our bikes created a sense of camaraderie. It gives members time to stop for a brew along the way and to chat and connect.

I did my research on the existing motorcycle clubs around Australia until I found one that had a purpose and mission aligned with mine.

I shared my vision with my mate Kev (aka SPOOK) and he loved it.

I shared it with my neighbour (aka MACCA), an Air Force Veteran with 35 years of service under his belt and he loved it.

He recruited another bike lover and veteran, his good mate, FISH.

I found what I call my "first five".

We had me, aka Big Rig, Spook, Macca, Fish and our L-plater, my brother in-law Midget. My tribe of five.

My experience with building teams and tribes is that you need your "first five" to help you form a bedrock for your vision and your game plan.

Those five people who believe in what you believe in as passionately as you do, they become your tribal leaders. They become your brand champions. They're your 'founding members'.

From there, your social network widens as your tribe reinforces your message and they turn into raving fans and advocates of you and your vision.

Think of all the great sporting teams and you'll notice a five in there somewhere. Basketball has a starting five. Rugby has a tight five in the scrum.

In our case, our first five quickly grew to 15 when ten Kiwi veterans joined us after our first ride. From there, we expanded into hundreds of members within the first 18 months.

The tribe of five with a shared vision multiplied into an army of advocates for our cause.

As our Club was originally established on the East coast, we had to go through the process of creating the Club here in Western Australia.

That meant writing our Constitution, incorporating the Club, setting up a Committee and seeking approvals from *both* sides of the law.

Before we could do our first ride, we needed to inform the fulltime, '1% er' bikie clubs.

That's how Kev and I ended up back to back in that carpark, surrounded by bikies. We needed the support and sign-off of the "1% Clubs" so they didn't see us as some new rival gang encroaching on their hard-won turf.

The existing clubs and "1 Percenters" had no problem with us and our mission and gave us the green light to **establish our place and carve out a patch of our own**.

The patch design represented the three arms of our defence: Army (Rifle), Air Force (Jet) and Navy (Anchor). In the middle was the federation star.

The meaning wasn't in the design itself – it's what the patch represented.

Our patch was one that symbolised service, sacrifice and freedom.

One that would mean we stand for war veterans. One that said we were the kind of men and women who had put our lives on the line for others and we would always have each other's back.

Finding your patch can mean a few different things. It can mean finding your tribe, that group of people who understand who you truly are.

But it's also about finding something to **believe** in, to give you purpose and to set your **compelling vision**, one of the critical elements to reversing the rut.

It represents what you're here to do on this earth. It's the reason you get out of bed in the morning and feel inspired to chase your dreams.

Your patch is your north star.

A patch is a symbol of everything you believe. It's the space you want to play in, which means something to you.

For me, that motorcycle club patch was the symbol of everything I cared about and stood for. It was also a visible sign to the world that we were the Club that rode for the military.

That patch and our new Club was part of my identity in more ways than one. It helped me through a stage in my life where I was feeling a lack of purpose and the grooves of my rut were forming.

Being future focused on this compelling vision that had my **attention**, created new experiences that yanked me out of my stale, day-to-day routine.

Having other people around you on the same journey is vital. Kev was that person for me.

Kev was part of my tribe and he was on board with my vision. We were standing in the same 'patch', wearing the same patch and sharing that future vision. We had created a sense of belonging and community.

When you look back through time, for thousands of years, humans have been using symbols (patches are the modern-day version) as a way to communicate.

Right from the earliest recordings of simple figures on cave walls, we've used symbols to portray a more significant and deeper meaning.

In modern-day times, logos are a symbol of what a business or brand represents.

It's the unspoken message behind the brand. The soul of the business. The values that it embraces.

When you wear a Harley jacket, you're rebellious. When you use an Apple iPhone, you're hip, cool and progressive. When you see Disney's sparkling Cinderella castle and the swirl that envelops it, you're dreamers. You feel the excitement and romance of the adventures to come.

In fact, irresistible and inspiring brands offer a kind of religious experience.

What is it about Apple, or other iconic brands such as Harley Davidson, Coca-Cola, or Ferrari, that triggers that religious experience?

In a study conducted by Martin Lindstrom, with neuroscientist Dr. Calvert, for his book, *Buyology*, there was no real difference in brain activity between strong 'cult' brands, such as Apple and religious images.

This means the memorable brands produced increased activity in areas of the brain associated with memory, decision-making, emotion and religious experience.

Lindstrom identified ten pillars that all major religions share, two of which are:

a sense of belonging and a clear vision.

For me, your **vision** is the most important of all for reversing the rut in your life. It's the mindset that believes that your best days are ahead of you.

Think about Apple in this context.

It's not just a tech company or a smartphone manufacturer. It's a social movement fostering a sense of belonging.

It's a company with a clear vision. Steve Jobs had crystal-clear vision. Everyone at Apple knew *they were there to change the world.*

Jobs had a *revolutionary* vision to contribute to the world by making tools for the mind that advance humankind. Everyone who worked there saw themselves as *revolutionaries.*

Which brings me back to finding your **patch**.

What do you believe in, what's your patch and your compelling vision for the future?

How firm are you willing to stand your ground and stand up for what you believe?

Maybe your patch is a cause you feel genuinely committed to.
Maybe it's your devotion to your family.
It may be your pursuit of a higher spiritual purpose.
Or it could be a combination of these things.

As humans, we're designed to look for signs and symbols. They give us a sense of connection and belonging.

One thing is for sure: we will never be the best version of ourselves without other people.

Choose your patch. Find your tribe. Map out your compelling vision.

You've now taken the first step to reversing the rut.

Ready to take some more?

Come with me, for the more you share in my experiences, the more the master life model and blueprint are revealed.

CHAPTER 2: YOUR COMPELLING VISION

Using as much creativity and emotion, I want you to imagine it's 12 months from now.

You're popping the cork off an icy Moet champagne bottle or a sparkling Kombucha bottle, celebrating a stellar year.

For the last 12 months, you showed up and you got it *done*. You reversed all the non-serving habits of your rut and replaced them with ones that served you. You made healthy food choices a lot of the time. You committed to regular training. Now, you're in the best shape of your life.

You set out to be the best version of yourself (a better partner, a better parent, a better business owner) and now your life feels *different*.

Most importantly, you have an absolute belief that your **best days are ahead of you** and every action you have taken is one step closer to that desired reality.

How fulfilling does it feel? How much more are you engaged and truly present with your loved ones? How are your energy levels? What are you talking about? What are you wearing?

Maybe you're slipping into that beautiful black dress you only wore before you had kids.

You're reading stories to your kids when you used to fob them off.

You're flexing your muscles and they look *buff*. All your mates are high fiving you for the effort you've made.

The past year, you've nailed it on the career and business front. You made the calls, nurtured the clients and made some innovative decisions.

You also made time to give back to the community and contribute to causes that light you up.

How does this make you feel? How many people have you helped? Where did you volunteer your time? What donations did you make? How many lives did you change?

While you were out there being the very best version of yourself in all areas of your life, you managed a fantastic work/life balance and travelled to many places around the world.

Where did you go? What did you experience?

When you do this above visualization and see and feel yourself being the best version of yourself in all areas of your life, you'll find the momentum to keep pressing play on your dreams.

More than just dreaming and fantasising, you need to *feel* the emotions that go with each experience as if you've already achieved them. Emotion builds motion.

This dreaming process is called **Gratitude 2.0**. We'll examine this powerful skill in a later chapter in Part 2, but for now, understand that this process is required to switch on your desire to achieve a life by design.

If you're feeling it, good: you're on your way. It's a critical building block.

It's the cornerstone upon which you build your magnificent life.

If you did all of this in 12 months, it's because you identified your **compelling vision** and **found your patch**.

Why is finding your patch and compelling vision so critical to reversing the rut and achieving success in all areas of your life?

Because unless you know where you're going, any path or method will take you there, which is nowhere on purpose.

Unless you're driven and inspired by a compelling vision for your future, you'll revert to the mindset that your best days are behind you.

You'll continue to repeat behaviours that hold you back, the ones that keep you in your comfort zone and stop you from achieving all that you desire and continue grinding out a deeper rut paved with the same old tiles.

My **compelling vision to support veterans and build a club** where members felt like they belonged made me spring out of bed in the morning. It meant I had to find the courage to overcome my fears and to step into the unfamiliar world of 1% clubs and bikers and fight (not literally) for what I believed in, no matter what. More importantly, it created the new conditions that broke the downward spiral of my rut.

My **compelling vision of having the No 1 real estate office in Australia** is what drove me to learn and grow as a leader, work long hours, study with the top coaches and mentors and sacrifice my family time.

Being No 1 in the game meant so much to my family and me, so it compelled me to pursue my vision. It meant more income, more freedom, more choices, more opportunities to live life on our terms.

It's that burning desire to create a better future for yourself, your family and those that you care about that motivates you to change, to grow and take the steps into the scary unknown.

It's in that place where you find all your future possibilities. It's where the ladder upon which you'll climb out of your rut rests.

It starts with the belief and mindset that **your best days are ahead of you.**

That's what ultimately drives our success and helps us become the best version of ourselves.

Let's dig a bit deeper into this.

Moving towards a compelling vision is going to require *change*. Change is uncomfortable, yet necessary if you want to reverse the rut and to achieve outstanding results.

Change isn't easy, but it's worth it if you want to be able to craft your desirable and compelling future.

We have to go through the gritty growing pains to experience the delightful rewards of a better future.

As one of my mentors, Robin Sharma, says:

"All change is hard at first, messy in the middle and beautiful in the end."

So how do we change? Well, there are some standard methods.

The first is through a major life event or 'epiphany.'
This can take the shape of a sudden death of someone close to you, an unfavourable health diagnosis (you or someone you love), hitting rock bottom in your personal or professional life, or becoming so disgusted with self-destructive habits (drinking, drugs, gambling) that you decide it's time to *change*.

Often this change is forced upon you by circumstances or external factors beyond your control. When significant events happen, change is the inevitable result. Usually, change has to happen immediately as it can literally mean life or death.

The second source of change comes from environmental factors.
Your physical surroundings have a significant impact on your habits and routines. Where you live, where you work and who you hang out with, all play a role in who you are and what you experience in life.

If you want to reverse the rut and become a healthier version of yourself, instead of hanging out at the pub with your drinking buddies several nights per week, you might join a sporting club or gym. You'll start connecting with people who place top priority on fitness and health.

If you want to reverse the rut and earn more money, you might surround yourself with people who are smart with money and find it exciting to make more of it, rather than people who have money blocks and always complain about never having enough.

The final method of change is through baby steps.
Sometimes it's the small, incremental steps that make the biggest difference of all.

Say you wanted to run a marathon, but you haven't donned your sneakers and running get-up since Phys Ed in high school. Going for a 5km run straight off the bat is probably not going to work out too well for you.

But what if you start with a 15-minute walk every day for a week?

Then, next week – walk for 30 minutes each time and quicken the pace a little. The following two weeks make it a slow jog with a few walking breaks in between. Watch how you go. I'll bet by the end of the month, you'll be able to jog 5km and it will feel more relaxed than you expected.

From there, you can build up to 10km. 12km. 15km. 18km. With this sort of baby step approach, running a half marathon or marathon in 6 months could be within your reach.

My client, Jacqui Jubb, did precisely that.

A 40-year old Mum of three, she decided she wanted to reverse the rut and lose the baby weight and get fit. She set her sights on running a half marathon, even though she could barely run 3km and she was 10kg over her ideal weight. This was her compelling vision. She believed her best days were ahead of her.

A confessed 'Type A' type (lawyer, writer, entrepreneur, and impatient to 'achieve' things quickly) her approach this time was different. She took the *baby steps approach.*

She put her old blue Nikes on and started to run to the nearby café and back. 2km.

Then she ran to the nearest beach and walked home. 3km.

The distances kept getting longer and she wasn't as out of breath each time she ran.

Before she knew it, she was jogging 5km without a puff.

Five months later, she nailed her first half marathon in 2 hours and 14 minutes and beat Oprah's best half marathon time by 2 minutes! #lifegoals

Reversing the rut happens for many reasons – environmental factors and baby steps are two proactive ways to approach change. Yet both methods are powerless without a clear direction.

As I said at the start of this chapter, unless you know where you're going, any path or method will take you there, which is nowhere on purpose. You don't arrive anywhere because you don't know your *destination.* You are too busy focussing on the good old days of your past. It's like trying to drive your car forward using your reverse camera.

Most likely, you're focused on previous experiences, successes or even failures and living in the past.

The side effect of this is where your attention goes, your energy flows and you can't create a new future while your past is draining you of your energy. You need it in the here and now so you can create a better tomorrow.

Your **compelling vision** for the future sets your direction and gives you the burning desire to change. It fuels your courage to do something different or new, by stepping into the unknown of the future.

That's why it has to be *compelling*. *Ev*olutionary factors will try and restrict you from changing and stepping into a new, unknown future.

To understand these evolutionary factors, we need to understand a little more about how we think and tick as earthlings.

We want to survive.

As humans, our ingrained, instinctual mode of operations is *survival*. Our ancient brain wants to protect us from the danger of the unknown and things that might eat or kill us.

As society has evolved over hundreds of years, there are fewer wild animals and competing tribes trying to kill us and yet our default instinct mode is still survival.

Your body *wants* you to stay in your comfort zone to avoid any unknown dangers that may lurk beyond this 'safe haven.'

Your mind, systematic thinking and instinctual behaviour are often the main culprits keeping you in the rut of your familiar comfort zone.

The way our ancient brain operates in survival mode is to have the maximum amount of focus and attention diverted to our conscious mind, so we're fully aware of our surroundings. It does this by automating any behaviours we repeat. It saves these repeating behaviours as habits in our subconscious mind.

Just think about the way you start your day.

Most likely, it's on autopilot. You get out of bed on the same side. You check your emails and social media before having a shower, a shave and eating the same bowl of porridge you have every morning. You drive to work the same way without even thinking about it.

Why? Because it's efficient. It leaves maximum energy and focus in our consciousness by helping us maintain situational awareness for the things that are trying to eat us.

But this is how we end up in a rut.

NOTE: To download a visual of the "Rut Model" and to leave a comment about your thoughts on the book so far, go to www.shanekempton.com/rut

We have a morning habit that gets us out of bed and to work each day, but nothing new happens. Sure, there are traffic jams; however, no tribes or creatures are trying to eat us. This is how we become "creatures of habit". We operate and behave in every moment from our subconscious habits.

The double edge sword of this survival mechanism is, that our mind doesn't discriminate nor distinguish between habits that are great for us and habits that don't serve us one bit.

Our mind just stores and saves all repeated behaviours as 'habits.' The sum of all these stored habits and your repeated and 'familiar' behaviours is known as your *comfort zone*.

Your morning routine that gets you out of bed and to work

safely is serving you well. The frequent consumption of a six-pack of beer every day on the lounge after work, or a block of chocolate every night before bed probably isn't serving you well.

Because you're repeating behaviours and routines that are known to your mind, your actions have formed a predictable loop or rut that is a monotonous life cycle.

Nothing excites you. You know and can predict the feelings and experiences you will have tomorrow and the next day. You'll be doing the same old familiar drive to work, having the same old conversations in the office and then numbing out the monotony of the day with your trusty six-pack of Heineken or block of Cadbury.

To your subconscious brain, this means you're *safe* – the ideal situation for your ancient brain's survival mode. This safe mode or your 'comfort zone' has a mighty hold on you. Any moves into the unknown go against all of your instincts and survival programming.

Change can be hard and this is why we end up in a rut.
Out of love and protection, your mind will do and say anything to keep you safe.

This is when you start getting the mind chatter like:

I'm not good enough.
Why change? It's too hard.
I'm not worth it.
Other people deserve success, not me.

Therefore the rut gets deeper and deeper.

Here's the good news: *Not all of your thoughts are true. You don't have to believe everything you think.*

We've been given the gift of free will and the ability to change our circumstances.

You need something to **believe in**, a **compelling reason** that gives your attention something positive and exciting to focus on. Something to override your default survival mode and shift you to a proactive 'thriving' mode.

So how do we make the shift?

I like to use my **3DA Coaching Model.**

> **NOTE:** To download a visual of the "3DA Coaching Model" and to leave a comment about your thoughts on the book so far, go to www.shanekempton.com/3da

It goes like this.

Dream.

Desire.

Discipline and Attention.

When we have a powerful enough "dream", or something we believe in deeply, it creates a burning "desire" within us to achieve it. This switches on our "discipline" to focus our "attention" on the behaviours which will deliver that future desired outcome.

You have probably heard everything starts with a thought.

Thoughts are like seeds. Once we plant those seeds and nurture them correctly, they begin to grow. When we nurture our dreams and give them energy, those thoughts stimulate emotions inside of us.

When those emotions are powerful enough, they compel us to behave in a certain way.

We are the only creatures on this planet that can alter our state through conscious thought.

We can go from sad to happy in an instant just through powerful thoughts and memories. In simple terms, it goes like this: first the Thought, then the Emotion, then the Behaviour.

If we want to change our situation or circumstances, we need to change our behaviours which are sourced at the thought level.

One of the most powerful thoughts you can hold and reference is a **compelling vision for your future.**

Your life can become very mundane and predictable, if you're only referencing and living your life via your memories and you don't have an exciting and desirable vision of the future you're creating.

This is the difference between a predictable life and creating a life by design.

You see, we are all going to arrive at our destination in one day, one month, one year, one decade. We can either arrive there by design or reach our destination with no design, merely making the numbers up in someone else's vision or plan.

A compelling vision is the first step towards a life you design (and not the default option).

Let's be clear: having a compelling vision doesn't mean you live your life in some 'woo woo' fantasy land. There are no free kicks in life. You still have to do the work. Instead, your compelling vision serves the purpose of giving you direction in the current moment to do the job efficiently and effectively.

To do this, the starting point for me and my coaching clients is to hold the belief that "your best days are ahead of you".

Yes, I'm thankful and humbled by what I've achieved and I remain hungry, but it's about balancing the right tension. You either live your life balancing your current reality with your future desired reality or waste the gift of the present, wishing it was like the "good old days" of the past.

Don't get me wrong. The past is a great place to visit but not to live. It's asking yourself this: who do you need to be and what do you need to do today to get to your desired tomorrow, while remaining grateful for what you have?

The secret is to *love the ride* and to *enjoy the journey*.

Rather than resenting the process, enjoy and embrace the work of becoming the best version of yourself and let the outcome take care of itself. You have to do the work so you might as well enjoy it.

You need to know what you want and go for it. The seeds we plant today is the harvest we reap tomorrow. If you want apples, plant apple seeds. The seeds of your compelling future are your *imagination* and *focused thoughts*.

You have the power to create an image or vision for your life. You can reimagine your future. Often however, as adults, we've had the imagination metaphorically beaten out of us and this is why some of us end up in a rut, stuck thinking about the good old days.

We get pigeon-holed into a specific role or job description or put into a particular 'box.' We're told 'this is your lot in life, accept it'. We're conditioned by the loudest voice and the most influential marketing commercials, telling us what's popular and how to live our lives.

Yet if we take some time to block out the white noise of this 24/7, instant gratification world, listen to our inner voice and connect back to our imagination, **we can begin to create and re-imagine an exciting future of our choosing**.

It's so important we do this. Without it, we merely exist. We don't truly live and we never unleash our full potential.

That's the good news. The bad news is that it's not all rainbows and unicorns from here. In fact, this is where the real work and the battle begins.

Now that you've begun to dream again, you will start to feel resistance. I'll bet right now, the voices in your head are shouting.

This isn't achievable.
Get real.
The economy won't support this.
You don't deserve that type of success.
It's all too hard.

If you hear the whispers (or shouts!) of self-doubt, excellent. It means we're on the right track. You are thinking new thoughts, stepping out of the comfort zone and into the courage zone. Now the work can begin.

There's no point dwelling on or worrying about those thoughts of self-doubt. It's time to step up, face and defeat your demons and win the inner game, a game you may have lost in the past but not now.

Using your best martial arts voice, yell the battle cry "WOTOWA"!

What does it mean? It's the transition from 'WO' (Worrier) to a 'WA' (Warrior).

Paraphrasing Dr. Joe Dispenza, our personality directly influences our reality. The metaphoric shift from being a worrier to becoming a warrior equips you with the mindset, strength and courage to overcome the tight hold your familiar comfort zone has on you.

To reverse the rut, you need to step into your courage zone. You need to be the warrior, not the worrier. Turning things around requires a *personality upgrade*.

I've invested three decades of my life, searching for ways to shift my worrying, self-restricting ways, to become a warrior of my life.

In the next Chapter, I'll share the insights of my discoveries and tips about how to step into the courage zone. If you apply them, you can fast track your reversal of the rut.

It begins with an invitation to a very secretive, centuries-old ritual . . .

CHAPTER 3: FROM WORRIER TO WARRIOR

The instructions I received in the mail were simple yet precise.

Be at the front door of the building at the address below at 7:30 pm sharp on the first Tuesday of next month. Further verbal instructions will be given to you at the door on the night. Bring this written order. Don't be late.

I'd been waiting for this invitation for several weeks.

Now that it had arrived, I was both excited and nervous. I was, however, committed to following through, because I was sure I could find the answers I sought within the inner sanctum of this centuries-old secret society.

The days seemed to drag out between receiving that invitation and that fateful first Tuesday of the month, but it finally came.

I arrived at the nominated address at 7:15 pm sharp.

To my surprise, there was no looming building – just a long, dimly lit driveway in suburbia, hidden in plain view for everyone to see.

I turned right off the street and pointed the headlights of my car down the driveway. I could see it was several hundred metres long, with a large gate about halfway along, which was open.

I proceeded slowly through the gate and into a large, poorly lit carpark. There must have been about 30 or more cars, many of which were late model, luxury European cars like BMW, Audi, and Mercedes Benz. I assumed there were men of power and success attending tonight.

I figured that meant that security was strong and ancient rituals kept tightly under wraps. It was the kind of secretive 'closed doors' approach that had kept this society off the radar of the general public for centuries.

Adjacent to the carpark was only one structure. An imposing two storey building with a plain ground floor, office-style windows, a solid Jarrah door and the feel of a business reception area. The second story had no windows.

By the time I parked my car and made my way to that solid Jarrah front door, it was 7:25 pm.

As I stood outside under the high ceiling of the porch, I peered through the windows on either side of the door. I couldn't see anyone or any movements.

My excitement shifted towards nervousness.

Where is everyone?

My pulse began to race.

Then I saw him descending from a large staircase towards the middle of the ground floor. A gentleman. A statesman. A man with presence.

The way he carried himself looked familiar. Shoulders back, no swinging of the arms, poised, controlled, graceful. With a deliberate purpose to every stride. It almost looked military.

He made his way to the door, opened a small sliding hatch at eye level and in a deep, commanding voice said:

"*State your name and purpose.*"

With a voice that sounded like a teenage boy who'd just reached puberty, I squeezed out my reply:

"*Shane Kempton. I'm here as requested. Here is my invitation*".

The small sliding door slammed closed. I heard what sounded like several bolt-like locks slide open.

Seconds later, the large jarrah door opened wide and with a gloved hand, my host gestured me to enter.

I stepped inside the eerily quiet foyer. I turned and faced my host and smiled nervously.

He seemed to ignore or dismiss my friendly gesture and made no eye contact. It was clear there was no time for pleasantries here.

Instead, he said: "Follow me".

He then re-locked the doors and walked back towards the staircase with that same purposeful stride.

As we walked up the stairs, I saw portraits of smartly dressed men on the walls from many different eras. Alongside those portraits were framed certificates signed in ink that looked many decades or centuries old.

When we reached the top of the stairs, similar-looking gentlemen were there to greet us, their faces emotionless and stern, again avoiding eye contact. They quickly formed a tight square formation around me with my original host leading the front of this serious procession.

As we began to walk away from the staircase, I saw something shiny on the belts of the two men in front of me.

A wave of dread flowed over me. These men were all armed.

I started looking for possible escape routes but could only see one – the staircase which was rapidly disappearing into the distance.

My mind was racing. Fear was taking over my body. It took all of my concentration to stay calm and reassure myself that everything was going to be OK. *Hundreds of other men have been here before me,* I told myself.

They marched me over to the far corner of the second floor, where there was a door into a smaller room. My exit was blocked, so I had no choice but to enter the room.

I stepped inside and looked around. It was a dull room with a few books resting on shelves and some hooks on the wall with coats hanging off them. There were no windows to let in the light, so it had a slightly musty smell.

My original host stepped into the room and for the first time, made direct eye contact with me.

I don't remember the exact wording he used, but he asked me three questions along these lines:

"Have you come here of your own free will?
"Yes", I answered.
"Have you come here seeking money and fame?"
"No", I answered.
"What are you willing to give"?
"All of myself", I answered.

He then said:

"Do as you are asked, without question and without doubt".
I nodded.

My host then turned and left, closing the door behind him, leaving me in this small room alone, wondering what the hell I'd gotten myself into.

I was left there in that room for what felt like an eternity.

Waves of self-doubt, fear, excitement, trepidation and anticipation raced in and out of my mind. Deep down though, I trusted my judgment.

I calmed my monkey mind and quashed my irrational thoughts focusing on my breathing – deep breaths in for the count of five, controlled breath out for the count of 10. Within a minute or two, I began to feel calm.

That calmness was shattered in a tenth of a second when the four armed men suddenly opened the door and marched in.

One of them said: *"Don't struggle. Trust us. For you are about to transition"*.

With military precision, they bound my hands behind my back and blindfolded me. I could feel the cold hard steel of a large blade pressed into my side. At that point, my heart was pounding hard, almost out of my chest. Fear took hold of every inch of my body. I knew I had to decide.

Either continue to worry about and fight what was happening, give in and say this is not for me. Or surrender entirely to the experience, trust the process, find the courage of a warrior and step into the unknown without fear and walk in the direction of what I was chasing, which was a *better version of myself*.

In that moment, I decided to **shift from worrier to warrior.**

I surrendered to the process. I decided to be here. I wanted and needed answers to the questions I had about life and I knew I would regret not following through with my mission.

I was in a very privileged situation. It's not every day you get invited into the inner sanctum of one of the world's most secret societies. My mind suddenly felt peaceful. I was willing to submit to whatever was about to happen next.

Holding onto that thought of a better future, I was ushered out of that little room, knife still pressed into my side, blindfolded and bound and led across the second floor.

After reaching the other side, we stopped. One of the four men knocked on a door.

A voice responded on the other side through a small sliding hatch like on the front door.

"*Who demands entry*"?

"*Shane Kempton, a free man, not wanting money or fame who is willing to give himself to enter*", my guard responded.

That response was echoed inside the room behind the door.

"*Let him enter*", was the reply.

I heard two doors open and they led me into the hall of this ancient secret society.

The voice of the man that allowed me to enter spoke again.

"*The man that enters this room tonight will not be leaving*".

With that, the double doors slammed closed and the ceremony began.

I am thankful for that moment of choice between being a worrier in my comfort zone or a warrior stepping into the courage zone, that I chose the latter.

I chose to be a warrior.

That night, I experienced an ancient, centuries-old ritual of dying and killing of the old version of myself and birthing a newer, better version of me.

It was a ceremony of good men becoming better men. It

was an evening of growth and learning. It was a journey of self-discovery.

I've always had an unquenchable thirst for knowledge and wisdom. I am becoming more and more curious, the more I learn. The more I learn, the more I realise I don't know.

Here's the critical point: reversing the rut requires you to *know yourself better.*

To reverse the rut, you must understand what makes you tick, discovering the "significance" of your life, so you can find the motivation to step into the unknown.

You won't make that first courageous step into the unknown or stay out of your comfort zone for too long, unless you have a compelling reason to do so.

This is why your **compelling vision** of the future is so important.

The gap between your comfort zone and your success zone, or what I call the Best Version of You (BVOY) is called the **courage zone**.

You'll find the compulsion to reverse the rut and continue to move towards the best version of you here.

You won't find the compulsion to take massive action in your comfort zone.

> *You have to take that first baby step.*
> *You must take that leap of faith into the unknown to unleash your courage if you want to continue to change and grow.*
> *You must jump before you're ready.*

Now here's a word of warning.

You may have incredible will power and discipline. You might force yourself to take that first step into the courage zone, only to find that the initial effort will only take you so far.

Willpower is draining and finite. Yet if you have a compelling vision for the future, it fuels your efforts and gives you the energy you need to keep striving forward.

As you're probably beginning to see, reversing the rut, success, fulfillment and becoming the best version of yourself is less about what or who you are trying to beat externally.

It's about mastering *yourself*.

Having a warrior's (not a worrier's) mindset and winning the inner game is the most significant part of the battle.

Every moment, we have the choice to be bitter or better. To be a victim or victor. To be reactive or proactive.

Or, as I like to say, to shift from being a *worrier* to a *warrior* (WOTOWA).

NOTE: To download a visual of the "WOTOWA Model" and to leave a comment about your thoughts on the book so far, go to www.shanekempton.com/wotowa

You may have heard the term "living life above the line".

At any given moment in life, you are either living above or below the line. It's also referred to in NLP (Neuro-Linguistic Programming) as "cause versus effect" thinking.

Over the years, I've adapted this concept and created my version of it, which I now use as my daily mantra. Many of my coaching clients now have it printed on their wall as a reference point.

The most important thing to remember is this: your journey to reversing the rut, developing a warrior's mindset and becoming the best version of you is about who you are *becoming*.

Jack Canfield once said: "*It's not the result that's important. It's who you become in the process of achieving the result.*"

We can amplify our personal growth through learning, applying proven universal laws of success and life rather than trying to resist or ignore them.

Contra to the famous saying, ignorance is *not* bliss. Unless we are continually evolving and growing, we don't stay the same, we go backwards and get left behind. The world is constantly changing and so must we. This is what WOTOWA is all about.

When we are learning, growing and evolving, it gives us a sense of significance and meaning.

And this is something humans crave. It's part of the framework we need to reverse the rut and live a fulfilling life.

When it comes to our evolution and that of the world around us, there are many different theories and explanations.

The one I like to use has five stages of evolution:

Survival – Meeting our basic needs. Food, water, shelter.
Wealth – The accumulation of basic needs plus some luxury items.
Power – Controlling those at the previous stages.
Knowledge – Wanting to know more and to understand more.
Why – Finding and exploring meaning and purpose.

From a world evolutionary perspective, I feel we are at Level 4, the 'Information' era. As a civilisation, most countries (not all) are going through incredible amounts of information and technology advancement.

Some countries and people are still in survival mode, trying to have their basic needs met. Others are fighting over resources and boundaries. In the meantime, however, most of the world is going through a period of massive information explosion.

We now have mobile phones that are as powerful as super computers, capable of downloading and uploading incredible amounts of information in seconds, all in the palm of our hand.

The downside of this rapid technological shift and information era is that it can leave us feeling vulnerable.

Unless we learn, grow and adapt to this changing world, we'll resist it or even try and escape it.

Some will find temporary escape through unhealthy and non-serving habits, like drinking, drugs, pornography, gambling, social media or gaming to name a few.

These habits leave us feeling isolated and put us in a constant downward spiral, resulting in a rut. We feel like we don't belong and our life lacks meaning.

Humans are pack animals and crave a sense of **belonging, purpose and meaning.**

When we stop growing and evolving, we can feel left behind. Working on yourself is a vital step in reversing the rut.

Being committed to continuous personal growth gives us a sense of significance, relevance and contribution to the community we belong to. If we refer back to the five stages of evolution, you can see we are fast approaching the tipping point from Stage 4 (Knowledge) to Stage 5 (Why).

We start to ask big questions like: "What is the meaning and purpose of all this knowledge"?

If you feel like you don't know where you fit in or you have no control or influence on your life, it's easy to slip into a rut of despair. That view on life could leave you feeling lost and out of control.

The lens we look through that influences the way we operate in this world is called your world view.

Your world view is precisely that: it's yours. It's not necessarily reality or truth; however, it's your truth. It's influencing your thoughts, words and actions (or lack of action).

Like my "WOTOWA Model", your world view affects the way you show up in the world. "Cause and Effect" is the critical principle in my WOTOWA worldview and I have used it to guide me throughout my adult life. This concept was a game-changer for me.

With the help of quantum physics, we come to Version 2.0 of "Cause and Effect". We now have the power to reverse the rut more efficiently and fast track the desired reality we seek.

Now it's all about *becoming the cause.*

CHAPTER 4: BECOMING THE CAUSE

I found myself in a rut due to an unhealthy relationship with alcohol.

I was never an alcoholic but I was a habitual drinker, using it to numb the challenges I faced during a tricky career and business transition period in my life.

I was a social drinker who enjoyed an after-work beer or two to unwind after a stressful day.

On the weekends, I'd have some more beers while watching sports with friends.

In my mid to late 40s, I'd just finished five years as CEO of an international real estate brand.

During that time, I steered the group through a major rebrand, innovated, overcame challenges, became the No 1 brand in many regions and introduced new technologies.

More importantly, I made some really strong, lifelong friendships (and a couple of sparring partners along the way).

All in all, it was an incredible five years and a time in my life I will always be grateful for. But it was during those years that my relationship with alcohol began to become unhealthy.

It was the typical 'mixing business with booze' type of affair.

Weekly interstate and international travel at the pointy end of the plane meant friendly greetings with champagne flutes upon boarding. Plus, I didn't mind the great food and the fantastic complimentary wines to wash it down with.

Meetings were always a lunch or dinner event, with a beer or wine to lubricate the conversations.

If they were successful, the inevitable whisky or two on the rocks to celebrate.

When I returned home from being on the road, after weeks of being away, the only thing to do was to relax with an icy cold beer and a few wines over a home-cooked meal.

Not to mention all the family and social events I needed to catch up on, which almost always included alcohol.

It wasn't long into my tenure that I went from being a fit, active, army reservist to an unfit, 20kg overweight CEO who drank daily.

Drinking in moderation and with the right intent can form part of a healthy and happy lifestyle. When we drink to escape and to numb parts of our life we don't want to deal with, is when things become unhealthy and can turn into a rut.

Once I finished up that CEO position, I had a business partnership that fell apart and alcohol became the soothing medicine that numbed the pain of the split.

Here's an example of an average day for me back then:

- Head to the gym at 5:00pm and work out for 45 mins.
- Pop into the liquor store next to the gym (how convenient) and buy a large beer to kick back with before dinner, then a bottle of wine to have over dinner.

- After dinner, I'd have glass or two of whisky as a nightcap.

I did this every day! It became my ritual. My daily habit. My rut. The things I just did *on repeat*.

Now because I'm a tall person and have a big frame, I carried that 20kg without looking unhealthy. Plus, I could drink a fair amount without feeling too intoxicated.

But my habit of having a few "innocent" (but regular) drinks was taking its toll on my life.

I was unmotivated and irritable. I woke up during the night, feeling parched and mentally stressed.

I knew I was drinking too much, but I justified it in my mind in any number of ways.

"I go to the gym, so I'm healthy and that offsets the booze".
"I deserve it. I'm successful".
"I like to work hard and play hard".
"You have to have a nice wine with a nice meal".
"You have to drink alcohol to have a good time socially".
"You have to drink with your mates; otherwise they will think you are soft".
"My ability to drink a lot defines me".

All these redundant beliefs were running through my mind and I chose to believe them. Yet all they were doing was deepening the rut I had created for myself.

Lucky for me, the catalyst for my change came from an epiphany.

Nothing hugely dramatic. I didn't hurt anyone. I didn't crash my car. I didn't get diagnosed with a tumour.

My epiphany came through self-disgust.

One afternoon, I was watching an AFL Grand Final football match at a friend's house.

We had a few beers when we arrived, then sipped on a couple of wines during the game. I then drank a whole bottle of whisky, neat, over the next few hours.

When the party finished, I got up, said my goodbyes and was far too in control for the amount of alcohol I'd just consumed.

The reality is, I should have been unconscious after drinking so much.

I felt utter self-disgust at that moment. It was the ultimatum for me to make some significant changes in my life.

No longer was I going to play the victim or be the 'effect'. I wanted to be the *cause*.

I wanted to become the cause of positivity in my life, not its destruction.

The next day, I decided to reverse the rut and become alcohol-free for one year.

To do this, I decided I'd need to apply all of the coaching and mindset skills I'd learned to my own life.

The first step was to write down all the reasons why I should stop drinking alcohol.

What it would mean for my health, wealth, relationships, career, my impact on the world and my spirit and soul.

Then I wrote down what would happen if I didn't quit and continued down this current path or got worse. (*And that outcome scared me*).

Next, I grabbed a journal and started to write in it every day. There were four headings I used to keep me on track:

1. Yesterday's wins.
2. Today I'm grateful for . . .
3. Today's intention.
4. Today's goals.

You can decide to reverse the rut in a split second. The journey of breaking old and creating new habits takes time and effort and I would need the help and support of my family and friends.

First, I explained to my wife and family about my desire to stop drinking.

Then I called five of my closest mates and explained to them why I wanted to quit the booze and asked them to support me in social events in staying alcohol-free.

Next, I removed all the alcohol from my fridge and shelves. I didn't want the temptation of reverting to my old, familiar habits in easy reach. I needed to make it easy to stay committed to my new routines and almost impossible to see any evidence of my old ways.

I knew it wasn't going to be a quick fix. It was going to take baby steps and I needed my environment, my surroundings and all those in it to support me.

Because here's the thing: It wasn't going to be the case of just swapping the old for new habits. I'd developed those non-serving rituals and routines over many years, so I knew it would take at least half the amount of time to reverse the rut of those entrenched habits.

The first 24 hours was *tough*. So was the next 48 hours. I didn't think I would get through the first week.

Two weeks seemed like a year away. A month seemed like a lifetime.

In the end, I took it moment by moment.

This was all about *becoming the cause*.

Choosing to be at the *cause level* in every decision of my life, reflecting on the vision I had for my life and asking myself in those defining moments of choice:

What would the best version of me do?

After one month, I had broken the back of my drinking habit.

By the end of month two, I had swapped my drinking at night habit to writing new material for my coaching practice.

At the end of 3 months, my sleep at night was deep. I wasn't waking up 3 or 4 times at night with anxiety and negative thoughts.

At the end of 6 months, I no longer identified myself as a drinker trying to quit. I was a non-drinker.

In the 8th month, I re-introduced small amounts of alcohol back into my life because I genuinely felt like a new man.

Now I can drink or not drink socially without it having any impact on my happiness or fun and it no longer defines me.

Although I didn't do the full 12 months, I had gained back control of my life.

I'd made it through a 10-night cruise, Christmas Day, Easter, a wedding, a concert and ANZAC Day, all without one drop of alcohol.

There were many lessons I learned during the above journey.

The 12-week coaching program I developed (The Best Version of You) was primarily built as a result of the lessons I wanted to receive myself and share with others.

NOTE: To find out more about my Best Version of You Coaching Program, visit my website www.shanekempton.com

So, let's dig deeper into the skills, mindset, and neuro-science techniques I applied to reversing the rut of unhealthy drinking habits.

The starting point is how you view the world.
For me, my world view is a simple one. *I don't believe in suddenly.*

Things don't suddenly happen. There is always a chain of preceding events that led up to each moment.

You don't suddenly put on 20kg (like I did).

It's the two years of eating hamburgers and fries and knocking back too many beers and long client lunches with a great bottle of red. It's choosing the couch, the footy, or box set over the sunrise jog or evening walk.

You don't suddenly lose 20kg either.

It's the 12 months of eating chicken and broccoli and heading to boxing classes and drinking loads of water and getting rest.

You don't suddenly go broke.

It's the months or years of poor financial choices, overspending, forgetting to look after your existing clients or failing to chase new clients.

Businesses don't become overnight successes either.

It's the years of long hours, meetings with the right people, getting clear on who you help, making sales, sacrificing family time to put time and energy into something you're passionate about.

So, what are your high-level thoughts on how the world operates and where you sit within it?

Does everything happen by chance? Is there some method to the madness? Is it orderly? Can things be influenced or is life a series of random events?

For me, **there is always a cause for every effect.**
This is how I choose to live my life: at the cause level.

I don't play the victim.
I take ownership of my life and the situation.
I control the things I can control.
My thoughts, emotions, attitude, and behaviours. I use these to design my life.

The body is your subconscious mind.

Taking this to a deeper level and following the excellent research and insights from Dr. Joe Despenza, you can think of your body as the sub conscious mind.

It habitually reacts to familiar or known stimuli, both external and internal.

What this means is that our subconscious doesn't know the difference between actual events that are occurring in reality and imagined or remembered thoughts about past events.

Our body reacts to the trigger.

We can relive and feel the emotions in our minds (both ones that serve us and ones that don't) of a one-off past physical event, a 100 times per day.

When these emotions are negative and non-serving, it's called **suffering**.

When we re-create or always remember a past event in our mind, it can trigger the same feelings and emotions attached to this event. It then results in the same motivation and behaviours. We will repeat thoughts, words and actions every day based on an event that happened days, weeks, or years ago.

It doesn't matter to our body (*subconscious*) whether the event actually happened physically, or whether it's just a memory in our mind every day.

It reacts the same way, emotionally based on the thoughts of a known and stored event (*memory*). This is our survival instinct and it keeps us in our comfort zone.

The good news is that we can use this process to our advantage.

Rather than habitually reacting emotionally to past events (memories), we can be proactive with our thoughts.

We can create, re-imagine or visualise future events we desire and experience the emotions, feelings and motivation required to achieve it.

Our subconscious mind (the body) not knowing or caring if this is a real event or mental rehearsal, will be compelled to behave as if it's already occurred.

You are now beginning to **Be** (think and feel) like the future successful version of yourself in the now. Consistently repeat this and you will eventually become that person and create the experiences this person deserves.

Taking this to a practical level, the typical model of Cause and Effect is waiting for something *external* to be the cause or catalyst in our life.

Now, by being proactive and not reactive with our thoughts, you can take it a step further. You can 'future pace' and visualise your compelling vision of the future.

You then become your proactive catalyst for the desired change.

Or, in other words, you are **causing the effects** in your life and not reacting to some external force.

> **NOTE:** To download a visual of the "Causing Model" and to leave a comment about your thoughts on the book so far, go to www.shanekempton.com/causing

To be clear, there are always external and internal factors that cause the effects in your life.

It pays to be mindful of these natural forces and universal laws that impact you and leverage them to your advantage – factors like the seasons of life and principles like sowing and reaping.

There are optimum times and conditions to be planting seeds (starting new ideas), working the soil (doing the work to the environment) and allowing life to grow (letting the outcomes take care of themselves).

When we work against the timing of such universal laws, life is forced.

When we work with these laws, there's a sense of flow in our life and success feels effortless.

Live a life by design.

When we start living life this way, that is **becoming the cause** and aligning to the external law of cause and effect. We start **living a life by design**.

In simple terms, we shift from a life that's predictable, to one we have purposefully created.

No longer are our behaviours based purely on our past experiences.

No longer are our habits simply aligning with our current environment.

No longer is our life governed and restricted by our rut.

We proactively create our desired future reality through

focused thoughts. We start to seek out the environmental conditions to manifest our dreams and live out the best vision for our life.

Go back to your compelling vision.

Life becomes predictable unless a compelling vision of the future inspires you.

Without that compelling vision of the future, we live our lives in the past, thinking the best days are behind us.

The term 'rut' means we have no compulsion to move forward in our preferred direction. We are stuck on a path that may not be serving us.

Thankfully, there's an ancient, proven method of breaking this 'doom loop' and the cycle of "same stuff, different day". The Master Life Model reverses the rut and Best Version of You Blueprint unleashes your full potential.

That's what I want to help you do and what we dive into in Part 2. Once you understand the critical importance of a compelling vision (and you've mapped it out in detail), the next step is to proactively focus on the thoughts of that vision so you can become the cause of your life.

That's when you're prepared to win.

Now, we need the **plan to win**.

A **focused game plan** is the next step in this success triad.

Ready to reverse the rut and lock down your focused game plan?

Stick with me and hold onto your hat.

Let's go.

CHAPTER 5: FOCUSED GAME PLAN

When we fail to plan, we plan to fail.

I'm sure we've all heard this before.

But I learned this lesson the hard way, and it still makes me emotional.

I first got into real estate by chance.

As a young 20-year old, my wife and I built a set of two units and went halves in the cost with my uncle.

We were searching for an agent to sell them and finally settled on a guy called Geoff.

Geoff saw something in me and said: *"Why don't you come work for me and sell them yourself"?*

That's how my career in real estate began.

A former SASR Soldier, he quickly became my first real mentor and not just a boss.

Having grown up without a father, having an influential male mentor in my life appealed to me.

He introduced me to a world of high discipline, physical fitness and the benefits of personal development.

I was impressionable and I found myself wanting to be like him.

I began to dress like Geoff. Say the scripts like Geoff. Use the same body language as Geoff.

Anything I could mimic, I did.

I was like an exact version of him except for two factors: one, I was taller and two, I wasn't getting the same results or success. I wasn't selling anything!

One day, Geoff pulled me aside and said, "Stop being like me Shane and start being you".

It was the best advice and it worked.

I still used similar scripts to Geoff but infused them with my personality.

Before that advice, I'm sure people thought, "Shane's a nice guy, but something is *not quite right*" and they were right.

When I started to be me, clients could sense a more authentic, aligned person and they felt more comfortable working with me and I felt way more like myself.

From that day onwards, I started to win a stack of sales awards and make more money than my family or I had ever seen. My confidence and ego grew along with my income.

But although business was booming and I was a rising star that was growing in income, my belief system was not.

I had a broke mindset earning a successful person's income.

As a result, I spent that money as quickly as I earned it.

I enjoyed long boozy lunches and took loans out on fast sports cars, thinking the cash would flow freely forever.

That was in the mid 90s in Western Australia. The property market took a nosedive and interest rates went through the roof (like 18% interest on my car loan – remember those days?).

So, there I was. High debt, high income, but living on a knife's edge, only just balancing the books. My first rut was forming.

A competing real estate office approached me with an attractive offer.

A slight increase in commission and the chance to be the sales manager of their new office.

This meant the prestige of a job title and a pay rise I thought I deserved and the opportunity to work a little less hard for a similar income.

So, I handed in my resignation to my boss and mentor and jumped ship.

I was under the illusion that the grass was greener on the other side of the fence.

I couldn't have been more wrong.

My new agency didn't open their new office in the timeframes promised. I was struggling to sell properties without a base to work from.

I had zero support and the market was taking a nosedive. My rut was deepening.

Soon there was barely a month's income left in my bank account.

I still had the debt but not the income to support it.

After a couple of months, I swallowed my pride and went back to my original boss and mentor and said, "Geoff, I stuffed up, I'm going broke. What should I do"? Without batting an eyelid, he said: "Shane, you need to learn about discipline and loyalty. Go join the Army".

So, I did.

I sold the sports cars and the house, both at a massive shortfall and I had no means to pay this debt back.

At the age of 24, I declared myself bankrupt.

My ego was shattered. All that success vanished overnight. I realised how low I had sunk.

I was like a shooting star. Burning brightly at first, but within four years, I had completely fizzled out.

To add to my predicament, I was overweight and my "Body Mass Index" (BMI) didn't meet the Army recruitment guidelines.

Although I was playing A Grade Basketball and I was reasonably fit, at 193cm, my 107kg was 17kg outside of the 90kg maximum weight required for me to sign up.

I needed to lose this weight to get into the Army and I needed to lose it now.

I'd lost my way. My new vision was to get into the Army and learn how to live a disciplined life.

I had a compelling vision and now I needed the focused game plan to achieve it.

Unlike my real estate career, I started this weight loss journey with a clear plan.

I used a straightforward formula: to go from X to Y by Z.

Or in actual terms, from 107kg to 90kg by 10th May. I had ten weeks to lose 17 kilos.

That meant I had to lose a minimum of 1.7kg per week.

I calculated what my food intake was for each day and at every meal.

I knew exactly how many calories I had to burn each day and I had every incentive to do this.

My wife and I had our first child together, our daughter Courtney, so now I had a family to support.

I had no job prospects, no car and we were living at my sister's and brother-in-laws' home and then at Lara's Mum and Stepdad's home.

What I did have, was a **compelling vision for the future,** which was to get into the Army and then the SASR and a

focused game plan to overcome the only obstacle stopping me: my weight.

I trained hard every day.

Ran 5km in the morning and then pumped out a gym workout in the evening.

I read and studied every little thing I could about the Army, the SASR and the Australian Military, fuelling my desire and motivation even more.

I learned more about my Grandfather's time in service as a World War 2 veteran and developed a sincere appreciation for the sacrifices that generation made to defend our country. I steered clear of alcohol and I ate a strict calorie-controlled diet.

I was *obsessed*. Without me knowing it, this was the genesis of the first step in reversing the rut.

So, if you have a compelling vision for your future, become *obsessed* with it.

I always link it back to my 3DA model – **Dream. Desire. Discipline. Attention.**

A goal without a plan is just a wish. You need the discipline to follow through and execute on that vision.

The 10th May finally came around.

The morning of the weigh-in, I shaved every inch of hair off my body, went to the gym, did an intense workout and then had a sauna afterward.

Although I was fit, I didn't feel at optimum health. My family said I looked sickly, but I was utterly determined to make weight.

When I arrived at the recruitment centre, they ushered me off to the examination room, where I stripped down to my jocks and jumped on the scales.

I couldn't look. I was petrified.

I heard the recruitment officer say "92kg". I was shattered. I was too heavy for the Army.

In the room, someone was representing all three departments of our Defence Force: The Army, the Air Force, the Navy.

The Air Force recruiter said, "That's close enough for us. We'll have you as an Air Force Defence Guard".

The Army recruiter piped up and said, "No, all good – we will take him".

I couldn't help but shout, "YES" and then quickly apologise for my outburst.

I'd finally made it.

Yes, I fell a tiny bit short of my weight goal, but I had been 100% dedicated to making it happen and the universe then conspired to help me achieve it.

Having a focused game plan felt *good*.

When you stick to a plan and it has a definite purpose and belief behind it, there's a momentum and a buzz to it.

You feel a sense of reward far more significant than you can imagine. This feeling is hope, which is the polar opposite to the feeling of hopelessness when you are in a rut.

It's not perfect though. It doesn't come without its sacrifices or compromises.

The next few days flew by.

Once we were sworn in, had signed on the dotted line and said our oath to God, Queen and Country, we were given our first order: "Be at the airport on the 15th May at 0730hrs for your flight to 1RTB (One Recruitment Training Base) in Wagga Wagga New South Wales".

Having now achieved my goal of getting into the Army, I spent that last night with my wife and daughter at my in-laws' house.

After bathing my daughter for the last time before I embarked on my next adventure, we both tucked her into bed and then watched the movie, "Ghost".

We cried together. Firstly, because of the love story and secondly, because I'd be leaving in the morning for 15 weeks of basic training on the other side of the country.

But for me, because of my vision and the fact that I knew I could commit to a focused game plan, they were tears of sadness, as well as tears of hope.

I was beginning to sense once again that our best days were ahead of us.

I knew in my heart that this next chapter would help my family and I reset and start over.

We could build on this newfound foundation of discipline I had discovered.

My time in the Army was invaluable. Throughout the remaining chapters, I'll share with you some of the powerful insights, tools and skills I learned and acquired that have helped me reverse the ruts in my life.

Needless to say, after almost five years of fulltime service, I was ready to head back to civilian life.

I'd reversed the financial rut I'd found myself in five years earlier and I had unfinished business in the real estate industry. I felt refreshed and ready to return.

I touched base with my old mentor Geoff and said, "Mate, I've learned about loyalty and discipline. I'm ready to come back and do this right".

Geoff replied, "That's good to hear Shane. You are welcome back, however, don't expect any favours. You'll be starting from scratch".

To which I replied, "Roger that, Boss".

During the next six months, I started to focus on my exit from the Army and my transition back to the real estate industry.

The Army paid for my Real Estate Salesperson Registration course as part of my discharge and journey back to civilian life.

I then embarked on a new focused game plan.

I was disciplined, extremely fit, confident, committed and focused on massive success. I wanted to support my family and make as much money as I could so we'd never have to worry about money again.

So, I started back with Geoff and got stuck into things from day one. I worked a 13-day fortnight, only taking a day off if I was told to.

I did anything and everything Geoff asked me to do and was a loyal "Company Boy".

He asked me to door knock an entire suburb of 2000 homes. I did it three times in the first 12 months.

He told me to speak to 20 people on the phone per day. I spoke to 30.

As a result of my newfound discipline and commitment, one of the side effects was success.

I won all the office and group awards and within two years, was promoted to Sales Manager.

This all felt amazing.

But there was another side effect and it didn't taste as amazing.

On the lead up to that promotion, I was running so hard in one area of my life (career and business) that I had neglected the most essential thing in my life: my family.

The tipping point and wake-up call hit me like a baseball bat to the head. I get emotional when I reflect on it.

It's when I realised this: I hadn't kept the home team advantage.

Having a focused game plan is nothing if you don't remember why you have that plan in the first place.

Without my family on board, my plan would ultimately fail. I knew something had to change.

CHAPTER 6: THE HOME TEAM ADVANTAGE

December 1999. I packed my military kit for the last time. Or so I thought.

In 15 years, I will re-enlist again but for other reasons (more on that soon).

I was back in real estate, this time with a clear game plan and a brand-new focus. I was disciplined, extremely fit, confident and committed to achieving massive success.

Since starting up again in real estate, I had a bright career and business vision. I had unfinished business in that realm (which was an ego thing) but I'd tell everyone it was for my family.

The problem was, I never actually communicated or shared my plan and vision with my wife, Lara.

By this stage, she was flat out looking after our three children, one of which, our youngest, Cooper, required specialist speech therapy in the city. Her plate was full, and she could have used some extra help from me.

I was too obsessed with my career goals to notice. I kept on running hard and pressing on, oblivious to the disconnect I had created in my family life.

I'd created another rut in my life, but this time, it was a success rut and it took a storybook to bring me back to reality.

It was 7:30pm on a Monday evening.

Lara had a great routine for our children. She cooked the dinners and did the baths and had them in bed by 7:30pm each school night, ready for me to read stories and say goodnight.

On this night, our youngest, Cooper, was in bed, waiting for his Dad to tuck him in, read a story and say goodnight.

As usual, I was pacing around, on my mobile phone, trying to match up a buyer and seller from the weekend to sell another home.

Lara had to nudge me to head to the bedroom to do my fatherly duties. With my phone squashed between my shoulder and right ear, I bent down, tucked Cooper in, all without missing a beat in my conversation on the phone.

The heartbreaking thing was, I didn't even see Cooper or the storybook he was holding up for me to read to him.

I was too immersed in my conversation. In making deals. In chasing the vision I'd set for myself.

As I walked out of the room, Lara was standing in the hallway. She looked at me, shook her head and walked past me into Cooper's room. I heard her make excuses why his Dad couldn't read him a story and she began to read him the story he so desperately wanted to hear from me.

When I heard and saw this, my heart sank. That baseball bat whack of realisation of priorities hit home hard.

It was that moment in time that I changed my whole philosophy and my Modus operandi for life.

I took that weekend off work completely. I spent the entire

weekend sharing my compelling vision and making a life plan for our family with Lara.

Because until then, it was only *my* plan. My motivation. My unfinished business and I hadn't brought Lara on board for the ride.

She couldn't understand why I was working harder and spending less time with her and the kids. The shift back to real estate was meant to give us more time together than the military offered, not less. She was beginning to resent my chosen field of work.

In simple terms, I had created a success rut based on ambition at all costs and lost the "Home Team Advantage" along the way. Without the Home Team Advantage, any career, vocation or endeavour is always going to be hard work and an empty victory.

Finally, I realised what needed to change. Now that Lara and I were on the same page, with the same shared vision, it was *game on*.

The timing and promise of the Sales Manager position was perfect and just the reward and recognition I was chasing early into my return to the real estate industry.

It provided the ideal solution to my family's lifestyle and needs. Up and until that moment, as a new sales rep, I needed to work hard to gain market share, sell plenty of homes and earn a stable income.

Being the Sales Manager meant I could stop selling all the time. I wouldn't earn as much, but the other currency I would receive in return was time. Time with my family had way more value than money.

Geoff put me on a mission to replace myself with three new successful salespeople – one to replace my market share in the field, a second one to cover my new Sales Manager salary and a third to make a profit.

I accepted the mission and began to coach and mentor the rookies in our office.

I knew only about one in four make it in the industry, so it was going to take me time, energy and effort over and above an already taxing workload.

But now I had the **Home Team Advantage**.

What did that mean?

Lara no longer resented the hours I worked because she understood why.

She was pushing me out the door knowing every day was a day closer to me never having to work weekends again.

I planned to grow the sales team from nine to twelve by the end of the year. It took me five rookies to find the three sales guns I needed to make a smooth transition.

Within 12 months of the night I didn't read that story to Cooper, I was the fulltime Sales Manager, just three short years from discharging from the Army.

This was possible for I had laid the foundations to reverse my success rut.

A **compelling vision** for the future. Something that I **believed** in. Something I gave my full **attention** to and obsessed about and thought about constantly.

A focused game plan to get me from X to Y by Z.

A committed effort through absolute belief in the vision.

Finally, just how Kev believed in me and our mission, Lara believed in me and our compelling vision for the future.

I had the **Home Team Advantage**.

Things snowballed from there. When Geoff took over as CEO of the brand, I stepped up to General Manager of the business, then Managing Director when Geoff sold the business to focus on his

CEO duties. Thanks to his innovative business ownership model, I was able to buy 51% of the business and I will be forever grateful to Geoff for that opportunity.

We floated the other 49% to 10 key salespeople, ranging in shareholdings from 3% to 8%. But being given the opportunity is one thing, making the most of it is how you truly say thank you.

I took over as Managing Director in 2003 when the business had a gross turnover of around $2,000,000. We took it to $8,000,000 in 2007 when I eventually sold out and took over as the group CEO.

Evidence is the loudest voice.

Proof we were on the right track came from the business becoming Number 1 in Australia for the group we were a member of, with six of my salespeople landing in the top 20 and two becoming national rookies of the year.

All the while, we'd created a high-performance culture, maintained our core values and made the home team advantage a top priority, as well as making lifelong friendships in the process.

My journey of success, learning and teamwork during those four years of business ownership, has created the blueprint for success and given me great fodder for speaking on stage. It has also formed the foundation of my work as a mentor and coach to my clients.

More importantly, it's meant I can help my clients reverse their rut, unleash their full potential and create a path to become the best version of themselves.

We covered this template for our business success in a workshop, which I still run to this day for sales professionals and businesses. If you would like to know more about this workshop and others, visit my website www.shanekempton.com

The purpose is to create a **focused game plan**, that delivers the outcomes of your **compelling vision** and makes it easy and straightforward to share with your partner, spouse or family (keeping the home team advantage).

For my real estate business, this meant listing all the suburbs that my sales team worked in, working out their current market share (we had 15 to 20% on average), and then future pacing our vision.

We built scenarios around an average of 25% market share in 12 months and identified what that would mean to the team's income.

We finally discovered that if we had 40% market share across all the suburbs we serviced, we'd make $10,000,000 in revenue. Using the same "from X to Y by Z", our goal was to go from $2 million to $10 million in gross revenue by 2010.

So that became our shared vision – $10 million by 2010.

We workshopped what we'd need to Do and Be in-order to achieve this goal and the decision was: we needed to become "world class".

Not a local corner store-looking real estate agency. A world-class, top shelf, uber professional and united team that delivered exceptional results.

We mapped out the details of what that would look like.

We created non-negotiables around behaviours, standards and to make sure we delivered a world-class service offering.

We got specific around what uniform to wear at different events, where to park our car when going to clients' homes, the message on our phones, the minimum amount of prospecting and lead generation we did daily.

The number of training hours per week and days off, right

down to the number of phone calls, door knocks and conversations we all needed to do each day.

Anything we could influence and control to ensure we were always world-class.

We even created a set of values with supporting and non-supporting behaviours to develop our world-class culture by design. The key to all of this was that my team created this and we all owned it.

They self-regulated the standards because they believed in it.

They felt a sense of responsibility to themselves and each other to do what needed to be done to achieve the team results.

When someone wasn't pulling their weight, they called that person out in the moment.

The critical point is that it was all **by design**. We were all operating at the **cause** level.

We future paced and visualised our business success and our ideal culture, then reverse-engineered and broke it down into behaviours that supported our mission.

The same can be done to reverse the rut and nail your personal goals, just as it does for large teams, businesses and global corporations.

It's all about the design.

One of the most essential ingredients of this success was the Home Team Advantage.

We made sure everyone was getting the home team advantage in place.

This meant creating a supportive environment and surroundings, where everyone has a shared vision. This included not only the team but our clients and suppliers too.

For us, it was about creating a "$10 million World Class Real

Estate Agency" that we all could be proud of working for, an environment of support, a high-performance team and an organisation that was humble, grateful and dedicated to giving back through charity and sponsorship.

For you, it might be something different.

When everything and everyone in your world is aligned to your shared vision and purpose, that's the Home Team Advantage 2.0.

Another important factor in our success and to reversing the rut was a commitment to personal development.

As the leader, I took it upon myself to lead the way and set the example. I was committed to becoming the absolute best version of myself I could be, and I wanted to share that with my team.

That meant reading books, attending seminars around the country and doing everything I could to soak up a vast array of knowledge and expertise.

My passion for realising the **significance** of my life and personal development was infectious and it flowed through to my team. They wanted to learn more and be more and this transformed my business into a learning organisation.

Evolving from a worrier to a warrior of life, I created my WOTOWA weekly e-newsletter to share this knowledge and my journey with my team to keep them inspired and energised.

All of this is part and parcel of the **Home Team Advantage**.

Yet reading and listening are only a part of reversing the rut and creating success in your life.

The loudest and most influential voice you listen to is your *inner voice*.

What you are saying and how you are saying it has a massive impact on the quality of your life.

I would go as far as to say that your inner voice is writing the script for your life.

Several elements of the Master Life Model and Best Version of You Blueprint have bubbled through to the surface of the stories I have shared so far.

I will reveal this complete Model and Blueprint shortly, but first, I want to share with you how you start to direct and star in your desired movie.

Do you like the movie you are in right now? Do you like the character you are playing?

The good news is that you have the power to change your character or the movie or both.

Let me share with you an example of the power and potency of self-talk and how it can deliver exactly what you're telling yourself.

It's time for Bootcamp.

PART II:

THE LESSONS

CHAPTER 7: THE POWER OF FUTURE PACING

My first day in the Army began at Perth Airport, Western Australia.

My entire family was there to send me off. My Mum, Nan, Pop (who served in WW2), my two brothers and sisters-in-law, my 2-year old nephew (who when 19 joins the Army), a couple of close mates, my wife Lara and our daughter, Courtney.

There were tears and sadness from everyone, but I also felt a sense of excitement and possibility at the journey ahead.

I felt clear and could begin to believe my best days were ahead of me, so I was focused and determined to be a good soldier.

A friendly, smiling Army corporal greeted us at Sydney airport and we hopped on board two buses with the words 'Army' proudly scrawled across the side of each one.

From there, it was a five-hour ride to Wagga Wagga, where another corporal boarded our bus and the reality of military life kicked into gear.

Unlike the Corporal who met us at the airport with smiles and laughs, this guy barked orders at us immediately.

"Get off the bus now".
"Form 4 lines of 12, 1 metre apart, facing the building".
"GO, GO, GO"!

I was allocated to Charlie Company, 11 Platoon, 4 Section.

Most of the recruits were only 18 or 19 years of age and struggled with homesickness and the gruelling routines in those early months. As a mature age soldier of 24, I adapted to military life quickly. I embraced it. I was thriving.

Being the second oldest in our Platoon and a little more worldly than some, I naturally stepped up into leadership and helped the younger recruits adjust to the army life. I excelled in most activities, but I was always keenly aware that I was part of a team.

Most days, you'd find me running at the rear with slower runners, giving them that extra encouragement to get to the finish line. My attitude didn't go unnoticed and the Corporals soon promoted me up the ranks to Second in Charge (2IC) to my section Corporal.

I trained *hard*. Really hard. Fuelled by my vision to turn my life around and reach the SAS regiment like my mentor did.

Time flew by and "March Out Parade" (graduation), was only a week away. Talk of who would win awards was flowing through the barracks.

They mentioned my name for "Best at Physical Training" and "Most Outstanding Soldier".

I'd worked hard and felt that it would be a just reward for my effort (*although nothing is guaranteed in the Army*).

In the Army, everyone is a Soldier first and then you have specialist jobs (drivers, cooks, admin, supplies) that support the Infantry. Before we marched out, we needed to nominate which Corps we wanted to join.

The best preparation to become a SASR Trooper is usually via the Infantry Corps and this was where I thought I would go next.

But my mentor had said that if I completed my basic training and my Initial Employment Training (IET) as a mature soldier, I'd be encouraged to apply for the SASR Selection Course later that year.

However, I would have only been halfway through the IET training for the Infantry when the SASR selection course was on, which was my desired destination.

So rather than choosing Infantry as everyone expected me too, I decided on the 4-week Storeman Course. It gave me time to graduate from both training facilities and to attend the SASR selection course. The perfect plan. Or so I thought.

When I told my Corporal I wanted to be a Storeman, he just shook his head and said, "*What are you doing, recruit*"?

I tried explaining the reasons why but he wasn't buying it. Being an Infantry man, I could see the disappointment in his eyes. He believed I was a competent frontline soldier and I wasn't fulfilling my true potential.

I decided to go ahead with my plan anyway.

At the March Out, I stepped forward to receive my trophy from the Commanding Officer and he said: "*Congratulations, Private. I see you have chosen to be a Storeman. What a waste of talent*".

Those words hurt, but my obsession to fulfil my plan drove me forward. There were so many voices and opinions trying to influence my decision, but I **had a plan**. I knew what was best for my family and me. I had to drown out those external voices and listen to my inner dialogue.

Then the military curveball was delivered.

Straight after March Out parade, I boarded the bus to the Royal Australian Army ordinance Corp in Bandiana, Victoria, to commence the Storeman's Course.

Upon arrival, we were told the Storeman's course has changed. It was now an 8-week course called 'Operator Supplier ' and wouldn't start for another two weeks. I was shattered.

I'd compromised my preparation for SASR selection by choosing the faster route of finishing the Storeman course. Now, I'd not only missed out on the valuable Infantry skills, but also the SASR selection course for that year. My plan had been blown out by 12 months or more.

I'd have to move my family interstate because the likelihood of a Storeman's posting in Western Australia was virtually unheard of. I was gutted.

My motivation to get into the SASR was more about keeping my young family in Perth and less about the role itself.

I loved the idea of being a frontline SASR Trooper but being in Perth was much more of a priority and the SAS regiment was the only fulltime Army posting you can get.

So much to my disappointment, we were posted to Darwin in November 1995.

I felt deflated. I'd missed SASR selection that year and we'd moved away from home. To top things off, because we sold everything before I joined, we were living in a place I didn't know, with no friends or family and we didn't even have a car.

It felt like I'd lost the home team advantage.

With no home allocated to us yet, we shacked up in the Darwin Travel Lodge for a week. We had to apply for a special $3000 loan from the Army Trust to buy a 1979 cream Chrysler Sigma, because the banks wouldn't lend money to a bankrupt.

I felt so out of control and powerless to circumstances, but the reality was this: *every decision I made led me to this very moment.*

Things slowly started to turn around after that week.

We ended up in a brand new, two storey townhouse on the Air Force base, with beautiful new appliances and furniture.

My unit was only a few kilometres away, so I left Lara with the car each day and I ran to and from work.

We spent our first Christmas away from our families and we felt sad about that.

Looking at my wife's face that Christmas Day, away from her parents and sisters, rekindled the fire in my belly to get us home and back in WA.

I thought that stirring feeling in my stomach was making my body shake, but as I stared at my daughters' wading pool, I saw it had ripples in it. That's when I realised: we were experiencing an earthquake. I took it as a sign we needed to move.

It would be 18 months before I would get the opportunity again to apply for SASR Selection and during that time, we adapted into Darwin life.

We made some new friends, Lara fell pregnant with our second child, Jordan, and we had visits from the family next Christmas. Our son was born and some family came up and visited us the following Christmas.

It was a great experience, but we both never really called Darwin home and never settled in. Lara was a young Mum struggling without her family and experienced some postnatal depression. Seeing my wife hurting, I knew I had to get my family home as soon as I could. I also knew the best way to achieve this was a posting to the SAS regiment.

That had always been the plan and I was committed to

achieving it more than ever.

I trained every morning and night. And I was *fit*.

I'd run or pack-march 10 to 20km in the morning before attending the physical training session. I even earned myself the nickname "The Machine".

During those quiet times training alone at dawn, I was applying all the personal development skills I had learned from my real estate career.

I had a **clear and compelling vision** to get my family to Perth.

I had a **focused game plan** to get as fit as possible so I could achieve that vision. This meant committing to gruelling physical training routines.

I was taking **massive daily action** to move toward my vision.

I used the power of a positive affirmation to motivate me and keep me on track.

On those crisp early morning runs and pack marches, when I was tired or needed to push through a pain barrier, I would visualise myself marching into the SASR Barracks, saying:

"I, Shane Anthony Kempton, have received and enjoyed the benefits of being chosen to attend the SASR Selection course, marching into the Barracks and getting my family home to Perth. The feeling of pride for achieving this goal feels amazing".

This was my mantra, my focus, my obsession, my everything.

My chance came in 1997.

I applied to join the 2/97 SASR Selection Course. I was one of only 150 soldiers, out of 500 who were invited to attend the course.

As I now had a date to work towards, I took my training to the next level.

There were practice tests like the 5km run, 3.5km boots and webbing run and the 20km pack-march, to name a few.

I was well within the qualifying times for all, and I had the basics squared away, but I knew I'd be behind the muscular Infantry guys who nailed this every day for a living. I'd even bought myself a shotgun to carry with me when I trained, to defend myself against the wild pigs and occasional croc you'd find in the Darwin bush and waterways.

But as with all plans in life, there were obstacles as well.

About two months before the selection course, I'd take a bit of time out from training and have a few Friday drinks at the unit's boozer (wet mess).

My tolerance to alcohol was low due to my strict diet and a finely tuned body. I recall sipping that fine tasting ale and it went immediately to my head.

After a few hours of drinking and laughing, someone suggested we head into town and continue the party. I was all in. The problem was I was still in uniform and going out drinking after hours in it was a big Army 'no-no'.

The others brought a change of clothes as this was their weekly ritual. But not me. I trained, worked, slept, and did that on repeat.

With my inhibitions down, I said, "I'll be right – let's go".

So, we headed to a backpacker's pub with a loose fancy dress party in full swing.

I joined the conga line dancing around the room and thought I'd blended nicely into the Friday night party crowd.

Crisp ales and conga lines turned into tabletop dancing

with a few mates and that's when a Cowboy and Indian Chief approached me.

The Cowboy said, "What the hell do you think you are doing, Private"?

"Dancing", I replied.

"Get the fuck off there", he quickly replied.

Being fit, healthy, invincible and utterly drunk, I replied: "Relax, mate. Anyway, who the fuck are you"?

The Indian Chief replied: "That's the Commanding Officer and you're under arrest for disrespecting the uniform, Private".

I gazed around the room and to my horror, faces became recognisable behind the masks and capes.

The fancy dress party was for Officers from several local Army units.

I was in deep shit. I jumped from the table and sprinted to the door, ran a few kilometres and escaped my pursuers before hailing a taxi home.

When I rocked up to my unit on Monday morning, the soldier on guard duty pulled me aside and said, "Kempo, you've been reported for drinking in uniform on the weekend and the Regimental Sergeant Major (RSM) is pissed".

Doom filled my body.

What have I done?

Have I ruined our family plan in a night of madness?

Next minute I heard a booming, raspy voice of the Regimental Sergeant Major and those fateful words: "Private Kempton, get your ass in my office".

With my tail between my legs, I marched into his office.

"Private Kempton reporting, Sir", I said.

In a calm voice, he said, "Private Kempton, you trod on your dick on the weekend, didn't you"?

"Sir, yes, Sir", I replied.

"Private Kempton, you have an unblemished record up until now. Knowing you are applying for the SASR, a formal charge on your record would adversely affect your chances. Therefore, I'll give you a choice. You can either accept a formal charge or accept extra duties. Which is it"?

Without hesitation, I said, "Extra duties, Sir".

"Smart choice, Private. You have a month's worth of weekend guard duty. Call your wife and let her know you won't be coming home for a few weeks. Don't ever fuck up like that again or next time, there will be no choice. That is all. Now get out of my office".

"Sir, yes, Sir", I replied.

It was a lucky escape, but not so fortunate when I had to explain the situation to my wife, Lara.

I'd have to work for the next four weekends in a row, which meant loads of missed family time. I had a lot of ground to make up for that indiscretion.

I kept my head down for the next few months, trained hard, put in the final preparation for the selection course and the day finally arrived.

We boarded a C130 Hercules Transport aircraft from Darwin airport; however, we had to stop at most capital cities, picking up other attendees along the way. The trip took several days, including a 2-night stopover in Sydney.

As several of my Army mates from basic training were based in Sydney, I decided to have a few drinks on the first night, which would leave me one night of uninterrupted sleep before we headed West for the selection.

About 10 of my mates met me at "Donkey's" house, not too far from the Commando Regiments Barracks where we were staying. After some catch up stories at his house, we made our way to a nearby pub for more icy beverages and bites.

As the clock headed towards midnight, we made a move to a local nightclub to party on, with many drinks under our collective belt.

I remember walking in, and the music was mind-blowing. It swept you up in its giddy magic and you couldn't help but feel amazing. The vibe and energy of this club was like nothing I'd felt before and I got lost in the moment.

In the best shape of my life, it wasn't too long before my shirt was flung into the air. I was dancing up a sweat like I was in the middle of an intense cardio workout session at the gym.

Unlike other clubs, there were no testosterone-driven egos or alpha males feeling threatened or flexing their muscles. The whole crowd was happy and dancing together and shirts were flying off everywhere.

Time disappeared as we stayed in our dark dancing vortex for hours. When I eventually walked outside, it was daylight.

We'd been out all night, just 24 hours before I was about to attempt one of the hardest military selection courses in the world. I began to sober up and knew I had to hotfoot it back to the barracks for some sleep.

As I stood there, bleary-eyed in the early sunrise of Kings Cross, I felt a tap on my shoulder.

I turned and eyeballed the shoulders of a very tall woman, who said in a deep, husky voice: "Do you need a ride, honey"?

That's when I realised, I'd been dancing shirtless for the last 6 hours in one of Sydney's best gay clubs.

Her comment and the whole situation made me laugh my head off.

I turned to my tall, broad-shouldered lady friend and said, "I'm all good thanks, sister". I hailed a taxi and headed back to the barracks.

After plenty of water and a good, uninterrupted 12-hour sleep, I woke up refreshed, ready to board the plane and head to the Pearce RAAF Base, about an hour out of Perth.

As soon as I landed, I realised straight away things were about to get very real.

Out of the 150 that got invited to attend the selection course, only 149 showed up. One quit before it even began.

We were ushered to a large hanger where we left all our possessions except the uniform on our backs.

They issued our training kit, radios and other clothing and equipment required for the selection course and led us straight to the swimming pool for the first of many physical tests.

The first was a swim test in uniform and boots, then treading water for several minutes before stripping down to your bathers for a lap of the pool underwater.

Those that had physically prepared passed this test quickly; however, there were a few who didn't, which surprised me.

Seeing the other 149 attendees in their bathers only, I quickly sized everyone up. I was one of the bigger framed blokes and the tallest by far. Most were around 6 foot or less, very unassuming and could easily blend into the crowd.

After a couple more running and physical tests, they loaded us onto trucks and we drove along dirt roads for about an hour or so, deep into the bush to our training base camp where the instructions and the lowdown on what was in store for us began.

Finally, we were ordered to line up in rows, strip naked and stand by for further instructions. A female Sergeant inspected our naked bodies before we got dressed again and I was sure this was designed to rattle us and make us feel uncomfortable.

The tests continued over the next couple of days. They subjected us to all manner of things, including sleep deprivation and constant mental pressure. The course is designed to filter the best of the best from the rest, both physically, mentally and spiritually.

By Day 3, we went from 149 to just 51 soldiers. Nearly 100 attendees had called it quits. Out of that 51, only eight completed the course and seven were selected.

I didn't complete the course.

Physically, I was above average and had scored the fastest time for the 20km load bearing, pack march test.

But my mental game was off. My reason for being there was my family and not because of my sole desire to become a SASR Trooper for the Australian Army.

In the chill of night and those long days without sleep, when I was physically and mentally exhausted, my brain kept asking:

"Why are you here, Shane"?
"Why are you doing this to yourself"?
"You are going to miss the birth of your child if you pass and continue this course".

My commitment wasn't 100%. I wasn't 100% committed to the task of being an elite soldier.

I removed myself from the course.

As luck would have it though, I'd done enough to show my potential and they needed the secondary skills I had offered as an Operator Supplier.

After a couple of interviews, some correspondence between the SASR and my old unit and a recommendation from my old RSM, I was posted to the SAS Regiment in January 1998.

So, had I achieved my goal?

Well, I had, albeit not in the manner I thought.

But I began to recall my affirmation. The one I had religiously recited for that 18 months of training:

> "I, Shane Anthony Kempton, have received and enjoyed the benefits of being chosen to attend the SASR Selection course, marching into the barracks and getting my family home to Perth. The feeling of pride for achieving this goal feels amazing".

I achieved everything I visualised. Everything I had affirmed in my mind, I had **future paced** the outcome.

I had unknowingly created my desired reality with that powerful mantra.

I never saw or visualised myself specifically as a SASR Trooper, but I had envisioned marching into the barracks and then eventually getting my family home to Perth and that is what happened in the end.

For the next two years, I served with the SAS regiment in my support role and I loved it.

Those that finished the selection course earn the right to wear the Sandy Beret. Those that supported them, like me, wore a very dark blue beret called the "Black Hat".

I didn't care.

I was a proud "Black Hat" and saw it as an honour and privilege to support and train with our steely-eyed warriors.

Above all, my time in the SASR and the Army taught me the

power of training and repetition. I would use these skills in my civilian life to help me rise to the top of corporate and business life.

Once back in civilian life and away from the Army, I was ready to recommence my real estate career, but I missed the camaraderie and the tight bonds you form with your mates in uniform.

Even when I returned with vigour to the world of real estate, I felt like something was missing. A lack of fulfilment kept me searching and asking questions and looking for meaning.

My thirst to find answers to some of life's big questions led me on a two-decade search for meaning and a higher purpose. I found answers from many different sources and gathered together the pieces of the puzzle along the way.

Yet I wasn't exactly sure what the end picture looked like until now and that's why I wrote this book.

My unique journey into many different walks of life and worlds has led me to an answer.

An answer to many questions.
An answer that has its origins in a deeper sense of knowledge.
An answer that will not only reverse the rut but will help you unleash your full potential.

Let's go deep.

CHAPTER 8: MY SUCCESS TRINITY

We all find ourselves in a rut at some stage in our life.

I've experienced several types of ruts, some of which I have shared with you already.

Ruts can creep up on you slowly and take you by surprise or hit you suddenly and they don't discriminate. You can be at your highest of highs or your lowest of lows and find yourself stuck in a rut, wondering how to yank yourself out of the groove in the road.

I've had several 'success' ruts in my time.

First, when I was climbing the corporate ladder, I became a workaholic and almost left my family behind by not sharing the journey and my vision for the future with them.

Then again, when I was at the top of my game, I overindulged in life's pleasures, filling my life up with fun and worldly experiences, crossing that line into a world of 'excess'.

Too much of a good thing can be harmful and we all discover this from time to time in our lives.

One of my favourite sayings is:

"Just because you can, doesn't mean you should".

Just because you can afford to drink a fancy bottle (or two) of wine each night, doesn't mean you should.

Just because you can gamble $10, $100, $1000, $10000 every day on horses, doesn't mean you should.

Just because your job doesn't demand an early start and you can skip a healthy morning routine, doesn't mean you should.

Other times, you might find yourself in a rut of despair, like I did after my business partnership failed.

Disappointment can lead to despair. You may have experienced failure and you've completely lost the motivation to stay positive and keep going.

A sense of failure rut can leave you feeling low in self-worth, like you can't get on top of life. You may feel like you don't fit in, like you'll never find love, or perhaps someone you love has let you down and you see no hope of recovery. Maybe you've fallen short of the kind of behaviour you expected of yourself.

I can recall some of my darkest moments with profound clarity.

Times when I've been brought to my knees at the end of my bed at 3:00am, naked, tears streaming down my face, arms outstretched to the sky, asking, "Why"?

Yet when I reflect on and dissect the events leading to those moments, I can identify the key thoughts, decisions and habits that lead me to spiral out of control.

Hand on heart, with all of the ruts I have found myself in throughout life, I know I am the sole reason I'm in that situation. I've either reacted inappropriately, behaved poorly or I've not been the best version of myself.

The other common denominator when I've been in a rut, is that my mindset believes that my best days are behind me.

The great news for anyone wanting to reverse the rut and turn their life around, is that we can solve problems and challenges caused by us.

There is a proven formula to reverse the rut, so let's dig deeper into the critical elements of my Master Life Model and the Best Version of You Blueprint, including what I call the "Success Trinity".

Most people have heard of the holy trinity of Body, Mind, and Spirit. My version of the holy trinity is Exercise (Body), Personal Development (Mind) and Service (Spirit).

I revert to these three empowering behaviours when I feel life is closing in on me, for they form the foundation of my Success Trinity, which I teach in my Best Version Of You Coaching Program.

NOTE: To download a visual of the "Success Trinity" and to leave a comment about your thoughts on the book so far, go to www.shanekempton.com/trinity

Let's take a look at these states of being now.

EXERCISE

The benefits of exercise are well documented. For me, exercise is one of the essential ingredients in reversing the rut and avoiding the potential downward spiral.

Firstly, I am 100% in control. I can choose when, where and how I exercise.

Secondly, when I exercise, it releases many endorphins in my body, lifting my spirits, reducing anxiety and giving me a better sense of self-worth.

Being fit and healthy and moving my body helps me maintain

a healthy weight, which again increases my sense of self-worth and self-respect and boosts my confidence.

You have to burn energy to make energy. Exercise increases your energy levels, and this is always a good thing.

When I'm not exercising, I feel flat and lethargic and it's very easy to spiral downwards further into that rut.

When I move my body, I have the strength, energy and motivation to push through setbacks. It better equips me to overcome challenges in my life.

One of the most significant benefits of all this is that when I exercise, I sleep better. When I sleep better, I have more energy and more mental clarity.

Often when we're stressed, experiencing anxiety or we're stuck deep in a rut, we suffer from a lack of sleep, waking in the middle of the night, thinking about the worst-case scenarios and everything wrong in our life.

Some of us reach for illicit drugs or alcohol (like I did) to try and numb the thoughts and sleep better. For me, alcohol made things worse. My sleep was interrupted, and my thoughts became increasingly negative.

When you exercise, it triggers you to eat healthier, drink less alcohol, think more positively and sleep more soundly.

You spring out of bed the next morning feeling calmer, better, more alert, full of energy and more inclined and motivated to repeat those same winning routines.

More recently, I have found myself moving away from traditional weights and cardio training and more towards yoga, stretching and bodyweight resistance workouts. I especially like the combination of mental and physical training that comes with yoga – a double positive towards reversing the rut.

When I finish each session, I feel alive, strong, fit. My mind feels *clear*.

With a more flexible body comes a flexible mind. It arms you with the physical and mental tenacity to cope with a changing world and the struggles of daily life.

Finally, exercise, especially for us more 'mature' people, helps with your sex drive. Feeling better about myself along with a healthy body and better blood flow, means I naturally want to be intimate more regularly with my wife. Yes, to that!

PERSONAL DEVELOPMENT

The journey of self-discovery has a dual purpose. The better you understand yourself, the better your relationships with other people will be.

It's through more profound and more meaningful interpersonal relationships that we solve life's biggest challenges. We need to get along with and understand other people to survive.

The more I learn, the more I realise how little I know, and the ruts usually form when I'm not learning and growing.

Humans are just hardwired to evolve and seek out our full potential. When we neglect this primary purpose, we often set in motion a downward spiral.

My development journey has taken me down both traditional, spiritual and radical paths all at once.

I've read and listened to hundreds of self-help books, attended workshops and seminars all over the world, engaged coaches and mentors, studied and applied many of the world's primary religious practices and beliefs; I've even joined several secret societies, all in the quest of better understanding myself.

When I put all the individual pieces from each path together,

I was finally able to create a map or Blueprint as to how to reverse the rut and become the best version of you.

But there was one book in particular that had a profound effect on me. The book was "The Da Vinci Code" by Dan Brown.

I read it just after I discharged from the Army. Although it was a work of "fiction", elements of truth were woven intricately throughout it and it left me with more questions than answers about the meaning of life.

If you haven't read this book or seen the movie which sees Tom Hanks as the main character, Robert Langdon, the Symbologist, it's about a man in search of the "Holy Grail".

However, rather than being a literal cup or challis, the Holy Grail is a bloodline. Robert's quest sees him dive deep into the inner sanctum of the world's most secret societies, following a trail of clues to a discovery that may change the face of the world's views on religion and our origins. The author's mix of fact and fiction is both highly entertaining and philosophically challenging.

After reading this book, I needed to know more.

Up until that time, I had never challenged my beliefs or perspectives I had on life. I was looking at life through the same lens and applying the same ingrained beliefs I'd inherited from my parents and my childhood.

I was oblivious, even ignorant, to how others were viewing the world. It gave me a greater appreciation of the importance of empathy.

The contents of that book inspired me to challenge my internal operating systems, review my definition of success and nudge me in the direction of living my best life, so I could positively impact the lives of those I led, both professionally and personally.

So off I went on my own search for meaning. My first stop was finding out about the elusive secret societies around the world.

Why were they so secretive? What was the attraction to the thousands of people who joined them? What purpose did they play? Finally, what, if any, secrets did they possess that could potentially change the world if exposed?

My online research led me to one particular society: The Freemasons and after a coffee meeting and several months of processing, I had become a Mason. While I waited for my initiation ceremony, I discovered another group: the Rosicrucians. Within a month, I had joined them too.

So, there I was, three months into my journey and I was already a member of two secret societies, discovering their secrets and learning why people are attracted to them. Finding out about the purpose they play in members' lives and society as a whole.

While it might sound crazy to some, the experience was fascinating and here's what I learned that I now use to help my clients reverse the rut.

There were three common elements:

- A huge emphasis on personal growth and development.
- A commitment to serving the community.
- Using symbols to communicate meaning and connection.

Service. Growth. Meaning. Connection.

These 'secret' societies don't sound so radical or secret at all, do they? They resonate with some of the more traditional teachings I dived into, such as:

Vision – The power of having a vision for the future.

Language – Thoughts are the language of the mind and emotions are the language of the body.

Mindset – Mindset and the power of positive thinking is critical to success.

Attention – Everything starts with a thought, so where our attention goes, energy flows.

Habits – We are creatures of habit, so you must have the practices that serve you.

Goals – Goals are great; however, they need routines and habits to achieve them.

Identity – Who we are being or how we see ourselves plays a big part in success.

Self-Talk – Self talk matters and there is power in using positive affirmations.

Courage – Gets you out of your comfort zone.

Lifestyle – Exercise, diet and a healthy lifestyle gives you the energy to succeed.

Again, many of the spiritual teachings I discovered had the same themes and elements in helping you craft the best version of yourself.

Look at what the core focus of some of the world's religions and spiritual paths are:

Christianity – Sacrifice and gratitude

Buddhism – Present moment and interconnectedness

Muslim – Discipline and routine

Kabbalah – Intention, the equivalence of form and the 99% vs 1% world

Freemasons – Ethics and rituals

Tao Te Ching – Awareness and nature
Rosicrucianism – Spiritual connection and energy
Kinesiology – Removing energy and emotional blocks
Reiki – Natural healing and energy
Metaphysics – Mind/Body/Connection and the 99% vs 1% world
Heart Math Institute – Global Consciousness and interconnectedness
Wabi-Sabi – Simplicity, letting go of perfection and finding beauty in all things

What's become clear is that in everything I have studied, the **mind/body/spirit connection** is ever-present, no matter what type of teaching or philosophy you adopt.

There was one particular world event which saw all of these paths of personal development converge.

Orbiting the earth, there are geosynchronous operational environmental satellites (GOES) that detect rises in the earth's magnetic field.

Several years ago, there was a peak so out of the ordinary, that it forever changed the way scientists view our world and the way we are connected.

But it wasn't just the magnitude of the spike that caught the scientists' attention. It was the timing.

The year was 2001, the date was September 11th and the time was 9:00am Eastern Standard time.

A plane had just hit the World Trade Centre. Now you may or may not hold stock in such events, but the correlation between the tragedy of that event and the spike in the magnetic field was undeniable.

It signalled to me that our inner world has an impact on our outer world. From there, I developed a new world view and began to create my own philosophy about how to reverse the rut, win your inner game and unleash your full potential.

The final missing piece to the Success Trinity was Service.

SERVICE

For me, service is the rent we pay for the privilege of living on this earth.

When I found myself in a rut, spiraling downwards in a doom loop, it was often a result of being self-absorbed.

I was caught in "poor me" or "the world is against me" or "why is this happening to me" thinking.

When it's all "me, me, me", you're failing to add value to anyone else's life.

Yet when I reflect on those times when I felt in "flow", "lost in the moment" and being "the best version of myself", I was focused on service.

When you help other people, you don't have time to focus on the rut or the sense of gloom you're feeling.

In my work with men's mental health over the years, whether it's with returning veterans in our motorcycle club or with Dads and blokes at my Steak Sandwich Men's Get Together, the common observation was this: they felt at their worst when they were *obsessed* with their situation.

So, when did they feel their best? It was during those times they were of service.

Serving their country, proudly wearing a military uniform. Providing for their family as a dedicated Dad. Sweating it out with their teammates on the sporting field, working together towards achieving a common goal.

In other words, these men all shone when their focus was on working with *others*, serving *other* people. It was the total opposite of the "me, me, me" thinking that can consume us all.

Often at our best, the "me" disappears entirely and we become one.

One team, one unit, one family.

Digging deeper into service, science has proven there are many benefits to serving and helping others, which are useful when you want to reverse the rut.

Some of these include:

1. **Can Extend Your Life** – When we serve others through volunteering at a community event, sporting team, charity or joining a not-for-profit, it can reduce stress, gives us a sense of purpose, belonging and contribution and may relieve any feeling of loneliness.
2. **Makes You Happy** – When we serve and help others, it releases feel-good hormones like oxytocin, which is linked to increasing your feelings of trust and loyalty. Hanging out with like-minded and like-hearted people makes you feel happy and content.
3. **Can Reduce Pain and Blood Pressure** – By taking the focus off our challenges and redirecting our attention to help other people, it can reduce the severity of health symptoms like high blood pressure and bodily pain.

Humans are designed to feel good when they collaborate.

That's why we've survived as a species for thousands of years. Our body releases hormones like oxytocin and serotonin, which create a feeling of wellbeing, as we work together towards a common goal.

As we achieve tasks and goals, we get a hit of dopamine, known as the 'reward' hormone. The flip side to this is that we don't feel too good when we're isolated from the above situations.

Cortisol is a hormone that your body produces in times of stress. It fuels your fight or flight responses.

We, humans, are pack animals, so when we feel isolated and alone, we feel more vulnerable and in danger. Small hits of cortisol for short periods are a natural human response, but it's not sustainable in the long term. Experiencing high levels of cortisol over an extended period can cause a sense of 'dis-ease' and then ultimately can lead to 'disease.'

What compounds this situation, is that our body doesn't know the difference between real or imagined danger or stress.

We can think ourselves into a state of stress, releasing cortisol into our body as the natural response. The consequences of this response over a long time, are that we feel down, anxious, isolated and sorry for ourselves, which only exacerbates the downward spiral.

We can *think* ourselves into a rut.

Now, the news isn't all doom and gloom. The very same conditions which caused your downwards spiral can be used to create your greatest success.

There is a proven model that shifts your mindset from thinking your best days are behind you, to believing and knowing **your best days are ahead of you.**

Using my Success Trinity as a foundation, I will share with you the Blueprint to becoming the best version of yourself and how to reverse the rut.

First, we begin with what I call the **Master Life Model**.

CHAPTER 9: THE MASTER LIFE MODEL

One of the key lessons I took away from my days living and learning Theravada Buddhism, is not to trust anything you read.

Do it for yourself and prove it by experiencing it.

I'm not saying you need to hang out with 1% Motorcycle Gangs, dive deep into the inner sanctum of secret societies, train with special forces soldiers or walk the path of many of the world's religions to discover what I have.

To reverse the rut and to maintain a mindset that believes and knows **your best days are ahead of you**, all you need to do is apply the techniques, routines and processes I offer you in this book.

But before I give you your Blueprint for your best life (**BVOY Blueprint**), we need to create what I call your **Master Life Model**.

The Master Life Model birthed from my 50 years of experiences on this planet has five key elements: **Causing, Belief, Attention, Significance and Belonging.**

> **NOTE:** To download a visual of the "Master Life Model" and to leave a comment about your thoughts on the book so far, go to www.shanekempton.com/master

When we have the right combination of these five building blocks, it helps you to both reverse the rut and lay the foundation for you to apply the Best Version of You Blueprint. Let me explain the five elements in a little more detail.

Causing

You are the master of your destiny.

Causing is all about taking ownership of your life, being accountable for your thoughts, words and actions and ensuring you have a proactive approach to life.

It's about choosing what you do, who you do it with, how and when you do it.

It's about living life by design and not by default. About not falling for the "suddenly myth". Living your life intentionally and at the *cause level*.

Externally, we align with the cause and effect laws of the universe. Things like gravity, sowing and reaping, giving and receiving, and understanding that for every outcome, result, or effect, there is a cause.

Internally, we focus our thoughts and emotions on being the person we proactively choose and not the habitual, reactive version. We don't allow our subconscious brain to drive our behaviours mindlessly. Instead, we awaken and become more conscious and mindful of our thoughts, words and actions.

Causing is about making a choice not to play the victim in life, being the effect of other people's influences and plans. It's about being a victor, taking responsibility for your life and being the cause of it.

When it comes to reversing the rut, this is the biggest shift.

You *cause* your life, either reactively and unintentionally, or proactively and with intention.

Which would you prefer? The decision to become the cause of your life can happen in an instant.

The processes, techniques and routines to live your life this way takes effort to master; however, it will be the most valuable investment of your time and energy you will ever make.

The best method for change is using the "baby steps", coupled with evolving your environment to support the upgrade. Overarching this approach is to ensure you identify yourself as this new person. We will devote a chapter to this next.

Remember, you can be the effect of change because of a reaction to massive heartache and pain, or cause it lovingly, through proactive actions and appreciating the journey along the way. The latter is aligned with causing.

Thinking back to my unhealthy relationship with alcohol, taking back control of my drinking habits, meant I needed to be at the 'cause level' and be proactive with my choices, rather than accept the status quo.

Becoming the number 1 real estate office in the country for our brand, meant I needed to 'cause' this to happen and not wait for success to roll around.

Losing the weight to get into the Army, required me to be the cause of every item of food I put into my body and the degree to which I exercised.

In all of the above examples, I couldn't just allow things to play out by chance. I had to take responsibility for my actions through proactive choices and being accountable for my behaviours.

I had to be the autonomous 'leader of my own life' to achieve all that I wanted to achieve.

If you want to reverse the rut or you want more success,

health, wealth or happiness in your life, the starting point is deciding to operate at the *cause* level of your life.

Belief

When we believe in something bigger than ourselves, we are fuelled with *purpose*.

We feel inspired by the thoughts of completing or fulfilling this purpose and we commit to the process and actions required to achieve it.

This level of engagement switches on our drive. It forces us to be disciplined in our approach to achieving this desired future reality, be it a cause, mission or goal. Our dedication and determination go through the roof.

It's all about doing what you love and loving what you do.

You are invested in the journey, as well as the outcome. You become immersed and attached to the goal and you feel a deep sense of emotional connection towards your purpose.

It means you *stand* for something. When you're in a rut, *you fall for everything*.

A compelling and robust belief gives you clarity on your vision, mission and values. Things feel genuinely aligned in your life.

Let's be clear: having a strong, motivating belief is not a religious term. Belief is an alignment with something that sparks your passion.

It could be for a better future for yourself, your family, an organisation, a cause, or even the planet. This is the "dream" element of the 3DA model we mentioned earlier in the book. The bigger the dream, the bigger your desire to achieve it.

Small dreams create small amounts of desire. Big, wild ideas and dreams stretch you to your highest potential.

The very thought of reaching out and touching the stars sends goose pimples down your spine and gives you the drive to step out of your comfort zone, into the courage zone of exciting possibilities.

Reflecting on my health goals, I had a passionate belief that a life where I was not habitually drinking would be a massive step forward for me. I knew it would help me find success in the other areas of my life where I experienced failure.

That vision, belief and process caused me to write this book and create a life-changing online personal development program (The Best Version of You), that would otherwise not have happened if I had continued to drink in the way that I did.

My belief that a career in the Army would help solve the financial rut I had created for my family, provided the drive and discipline I needed to shed the weight for me to join the Australian Defence Force.

Dream big, but here's a word of warning: when you do dream big, have lofty goals and believe in something bigger than yourself, you will create nay-sayers.

Don't listen to people who don't have your best intentions at heart. These people will be critical of your vision, dream and belief, because you might do something they're scared of or are not prepared to do themselves.

More often than not, the criticism is less about you and more about their self-doubts or insecurities.

For example, when we set our revenue goal of $10 million by 2010 for our real estate business, no one in Western Australia at the time (even rarely at the time I write this book) had achieved such success.

When we shared our goal with our industry peers, they laughed at us. Yet the whole team and I had an absolute belief in ourselves, each other and our shared vision for the business.

Had I listened to our critics and not believed in our vision wholeheartedly, we wouldn't have even attempted to achieve our business goals.

I probably wouldn't have written this book or helped the hundreds of clients we sold and bought houses for or helped all of my coaching clients to reverse the rut and achieve success on their own terms.

If you're in a rut, find something to believe in. A cause. A reason to get up out of bed and get moving. A better future for yourself or someone else.

Taking the focus off yourself and being 100% present in your service to others, is a powerful method to reversing a rut and finding massive success.

Attention

Attention is the beautiful side effect of believing in something. When we believe in a cause or mission, we're passionate about; it gets our full attention.

When something has our full and undivided attention, we throw all of our energy into it, opening the doorway for peak performance.

We are engaged, efficient and extremely productive. This level of focus brings us into a state of flow.

When you love what you do, you're not wasteful with your time, energy and resources, you get stuff done. You kick personal and professional goals all the time.

Regardless if someone is watching or not, you do the work because it's your sweet spot and passion. The effort feels *effortless*. Executing, implementing and even going the extra mile feels easy because your productivity is on fire.

Yet attention is a double edge sword unless we apply both causality and belief.

If you're in a big rut, your problems, fears, anxieties, hatred, jealousy, judgment, overeating and substance abuse gets your full attention. This leaves us without any energy or focus to work on solutions and or map out a more desirable future or better version of ourselves.

By giving these challenges our full attention, we fuel them even more and the rut gets deeper.

In these situations, we need to break the circuit of our reactive, non-serving attention and proactively choose to focus on more positive thoughts, words and actions.

As hard as it may feel, you have 100% control over this process of 'correction'.

If you are in a personal rut like I was and you're disgusted in some of your non- serving habits like drinking or eating too much, drug abuse, gambling, pornography or other types of addictions, then the first step is to stop identifying yourself as a person who drinks, eats or engages in substance abuse. You can then begin to direct your attention to becoming a better version of you.

When you catch yourself slipping into one of your non-serving habits, stop yourself by bringing your attention back to the present moment.

Do something completely random to break the circuits of your current thinking. Clap your hands, laugh out loud, slap your leg, anything to grab your attention away from your non-serving thinking.

Now, breathe in and out deeply, five or six times. Inhale for a count of 5 and exhale for a count of 8 to 10. This is a proven way to calm your thoughts.

Next, **become fully present in the moment**.

We can do this by sensing every part of our body from our toes up to our scalp.

Sense your toes, then your feet, then feel it up your calves, thighs, hips, stomach, back, shoulders, chest, neck, face and finally to the top of your head.

This will bring your attention fully into the current moment.

Now, create a mental vision of the you that you would prefer and give it your full attention. It's all about focusing your undivided attention on a ***better version of you***.

What does that version of you look like? What do you wear? What do you say? Who do you socialise with? Where do you hang out?

Most importantly, what choice would that version of you make in this present moment?

Imagine this best version of you with all of your heart, mind, emotions and soul.

Now open your eyes and physically make the decision and choice to do exactly as the best version of you would have done in that moment.

You can use the above technique in the moment of choice and as a daily meditation to help you prepare for these situations when they arise. Mental rehearsal is a tremendous pre-emptive strike.

If you did make a better choice in that moment after completing the above technique, reward yourself in a healthy way. This can be some encouraging self-talk or a treat like a coffee, massage or concert ticket.

If you didn't make a better choice and you slipped back into the old habit, acknowledge it and write down how you will do things differently next time.

Don't be hard on yourself. Remember: baby steps and change your environment to support the best version of you.

For me, self-doubt has always been my Achilles Heel. I've been plagued with thoughts of not being worthy, not being good enough and not being smart enough my entire adult life.

With my attention focused on these non-serving thoughts, my energy would always flow there. The side effect was that I would sabotage my success or limit it in some shape or form.

Worse still, I would mask my self-doubt and insecurities with material things, like sports cars and fashion labels to look more in control of my life.

Yet, no matter how many external things I had or how I filled my life with materialistic stuff, it never filled the void I felt inside of me.

That was my biggest rut. It's when I started doing the inner work that I was able to reverse that rut.

I've managed these non-serving thoughts of my rut through the above breathing technique, getting into the present moment, and visualizing a better version of me – someone who is confident, intelligent, engaging, entertaining, valuable, positive, healthy and wealthy.

I would open my eyes and physically step forward to be that person.

That, coupled with my positive affirmation mentioned earlier in the book, is my daily routine. It's been my catalyst to healthier self-worth and a more fulfilled state of being.

There is another super powerful way to use your attention: focus on **gratitude**.

I dedicate a whole chapter to this subject as this is the game changer to reversing the rut and achieving massive success in your life.

For now, always remember where our attention goes, our energy flows.

Significance

With significance, you continuously grow and develop both personally and professionally.

As a result, you are super productive, naturally reaching and unleashing your full potential. At the same time, you are recognized by your peers, your family and yourself for your efforts.

This is the ultimate state of balance, combining an abundance of ambition for excellence and appreciation of what you already have. In this state, success in all areas of life flows smoothly to you.

Significance is about fulfilling that intrinsic desire of growing as a person and becoming better in all that you do. You want to identify yourself as the kind of person who gets stuff done, ethically and effortlessly.

You understand life gives us not what we want, not what we need but what we deserve from who we are being. Investing in our own personal and professional development is the best endeavour possible. It is the ultimate reward for effort.

You, life, the world – we're all constantly evolving and going through the five stages (Survival, Wealth, Power, Knowledge, Why).

Within our DNA, is an intrinsic desire to grow and unless we are fulfilling this desire, we feel stagnant. It's like water that stops flowing. We become stale with no sense of energy or flow – we find ourselves in a rut.

When we can experience growth and are recognized for it, whether by ourselves or by another person, we get a hit of dopamine and we become energized about the future.

We feel compelled to keep going. That's our body's way of making progression and growth feel good. That's how we've survived and thrived for thousands of years.

We also know that dopamine has a side effect: it's addictive. As a society, we've created ways to become hooked on the experience of measured progress in just about every area of our lives.

Reflecting on my journey and many experiences, you can see how we have cleverly used steady growth to keep us compelled (or even addicted) on a particular path.

For example:

The Military – You move through a ranking system, gaining recognition for your skills and tenure along the way. The higher the rank, the more respect you gain.

Martial Arts – In most forms of martial arts and self-defence, there is a 'belt' system that demonstrates your level of skills and progress. From White through to Black (with various colours and stages in between), your training focuses on obtaining your next belt colour and each one represents what stage you're at. Black tips or stripes on the end of your black belt demonstrate your levels of mastery.

Sales – Most sales industries have some reward and recognition program (commissions based on sales targets, for example), designed to keep the salespeople motivated and striving for the next award or incentive.

Network Marketing – Similar to sales and the military, these organisations have ranking and bonus systems designed to reward you for the next level of success.

Secret Societies – The ones I was involved in had different levels of knowledge that were revealed to you as you progressed through each step and rank. The more you learned, the more they revealed to you and the more you wanted to know.

Loyalty Programs – Frequent flyer programs, coffee cards and other types of membership programs reward you for using and buying their products and services consistently. Every time you reach a certain status or bonus level (silver, gold and platinum etc.), you get your promised 'loyalty freebie'.

When we find ourselves in a rut, it's often because we don't feel a sense of progress in our lives.

So here's the reality of that situation: if you're not growing, at best, you stay the same and at worst, you're heading backwards as others around you grow, evolve and shift into a new way of being.

For me, I slip into a rut when I stop growing and learning. I become self-absorbed. I focus more on what's happened in my life and what's gone wrong or is no longer present in my life (like the good old days of the past).

That's the rut mindset of "my best days are behind me".

On the other hand, I thrive on new knowledge and experiences and love sharing what I learn with others. Learn how to *thrive*.

All it takes to start the thriving process is to pick up a book and start reading or listening to it. Watch a new YouTube video on a topic you're interested in, listen to an inspiring podcast, attend a workshop to discover something new, speak to someone different, travel to a place you've never been before.

To shake off the 'rut', do something that breaks the habitual circuits of your 'same old same old'.

When you're ready to take your learning to another level, remember that you don't need anything external. It's all inside of *you*. Many of the most powerful personal insights come from reflection and meditation, from that place where you tap into the infinite knowledge resource centre of your consciousness.

The age-old saying of "know thyself" is timeless wisdom, for when we become curious and want to know more about ourselves, we feed our intrinsic desire to grow.

When we become curious about becoming better versions of ourselves and growing as people, we begin to feel **significant,** the polar opposite experience of the 'I'm not worthy or not good enough' rut many of us find ourselves in.

As you learn and grow, listen and apply, your mindset naturally shifts and you begin to live your life, genuinely believing that "your best days are ahead of you".

Belonging

Humans crave a sense of belonging. We are pack animals. We've survived as a species for thousands of years by belonging and working together in tribes, communities and civilizations.

When you're in the company of people who fuel your passion and purpose, you begin to feel a sense of recognition for your efforts and inspired by the synergy created by like-minded and like-hearted souls.

A strong sense of conviction boosts your self-worth. Contributing to a common cause makes you feel connected to those around you who are all on a familiar path.

In this 'belonging' space, you can apply your innate gifts, use your strengths, work with people you like and trust, do what you love and be recognized for it.

One of our greatest fears is a fear of isolation. We can feel like we are in a rut when we experience isolation.

This can come in several forms.

First, we could be isolated from other people, living a life of unwanted solitude due to physical or emotional challenges.

Second, we can feel isolated when we hang out with the wrong people. People who don't support or appreciate our gifts and talents and don't give us the recognition we crave. It's hard to experience significance in this environment.

Third, when we associate with people who fuel our non-serving behaviours and habits, especially if we are trying to change. This leaves us feeling disconnected as we're not aligned with those around us.

To experience a sense of belonging, you need to surround yourself with people who believe in what you believe. You have to be clear on what you believe and articulate and communicate it, so you can attract like-minded and like-hearted people into your life.

Better still, be proactive and seek these people out yourself. For example, if you want to get fit and healthy, you may need to join a gym or yoga studio.

If you want to learn more in a chosen field or industry, you may need to attend workshops and seminars where experts share valuable information.

You might want to travel more and experience different countries and cultures, so you could join a travel club.

Once you're clear on what you believe and what your purpose is, big or small, seek out people who can support you in your mission, who complement your strengths, who believe in what you believe.

Remember, if you're operating at the cause level of life, you can decide in an instant that your current environment and the people you're hanging out with are not healthy or serving you. You can make a proactive decision to change.

Setting up the motorcycle club for veterans meant I needed to find people who were passionate about this cause, who rode motorcycles and were prepared to learn how best we could serve our returning veterans. I put it out there to all my friends and I knocked on my neighbour's door because I knew he rode a bike and was in the Airforce.

Once I had my first five members on board, we continued to work our networks as well as a social media drive. Before long, because we were clear on what we were trying to achieve, we attracted hundreds of the right people who believed what we believed.

Those that tried to join us for the wrong reasons didn't make it through the selection process or were quickly found out and moved on by the culture of the club.

Because we fostered that sense of belonging, that club is still going strong and continues to attract like-minded and like-hearted people to this day.

All those members tick off all five elements of my Master Life Model. They are purpose-driven, they proactively chose to join, they believe in the mission, and they are focused on the club's objectives. Each member is recognized for their tenure and qualifications, and they feel like they belong to something bigger than themselves.

Summary

This is my Master Life Model for living a fulfilled life, which is the very opposite of being in a rut. The five elements of the Model are appropriate for just about any person or organization wanting to see and believe their best days are ahead of them.

When a person has a sense of control or autonomy over their life (**causing**), have a purpose they are passionate about and believe in what they are doing (**belief**), that has their full attention with their efforts being channelled into its success (**attention**), they are growing and being recognized for their gifts, strengths and efforts (**significance**), they are doing it with people they know, like and trust (**belonging**), this is when they truly shine and feel fulfilled.

This Model is not just for individuals either. I've seen this Model applied in sporting teams, family units, small businesses, large corporations, in the military, social clubs, and many other organizations around the world.

When an organization can create an environment that promotes these five elements, long term success and greatness are easily within reach. If the people are great, the organization can be remarkable.

So now that we have the elements of the Master Life Model in place, can you see it has the power to reverse any rut?

Now we've reversed the rut, you can truly believe **your best days are ahead of you**, so it's time to lay the foundation for the very best version of you. This is where you get to unleash your full potential by applying my **Best Version of You Blueprint**.

Let's go!

CHAPTER 10: THE BEST VERSION OF YOU BLUEPRINT

Now that we understand the Master Life Model has the power to reverse the rut, it's time to unleash your full potential.

Think of the Master Life Model as the solid foundation upon which you build your success skyscraper.

Like any foundation that's weak or not deep enough, when the raging storm hits or earthquake shatters the ground, the structure built upon it can crumble and fall into pieces.

The Master Life Model is the solid foundation for your dreams, the pillars that support your goals, the platform from which you can see your best days are ahead of you and the rudder which keeps you steady and on course in life's rough seas.

With this strong foundation in place, let's build a structure dedicated to you, one that represents your magnificence.

Just like building a physical structure, you begin with a **Blueprint for your best life (BVOY Blueprint).**

> **NOTE:** To download a visual of the "BVOY Blueprint" and to leave a comment about your thoughts on the book so far, go to www.shanekempton.com/bvoy

My BVOY Blueprint consists of four pillars.

Compelling Vision
Focused Game Plan
Winning Routines
Massive Action

Throughout my life, I have experienced success when these pillars have been present. Conversely, when I have been at my lowest, many of these pillars were nowhere to be seen.

Let's dive into each of the four pillars now and see how you can apply the BVOY Blueprint to your life.

Your Compelling Vision for the Future

By now, you know that without a compelling vision for the future, our mindset can be stuck thinking that our best days are behind us, and so, we are destined to repeat the thoughts, emotions and behaviours from our past.

The belief and mindset that your best days are ahead of you starts with a compelling vision of the future.

That vision provides the courage for you to step out of your comfort zone and into the unknown, where you can find all of your future possibilities.

The times I have found myself in a rut were those times I had no belief in something greater than my current reality. I had no real vision for the future.

When I'm not in the present and thinking of some new and better experience in the future, my attention is stuck in the past. I think only of the good old days that are now long gone.

We must maintain a balance of being both ambitious and

appreciative of what we have, both humble and hungry, and being in the present moment with a focus on a better future.

Your compelling vision for the future can be anything that compels you to act. Typically, it's aligned with what you believe in from the Master Life Model.

I've had grand, long-term visions and smaller, more personal short-term ones. It's fine to have more than one, but I suggest not having more than three or you run the risk of spreading yourself too thin.

When I wanted to join the Army, my long-term vision was to make it to the SAS regiment. My short-term vision was to lose weight to get accepted into the basic training program.

As a salesperson, my long-term vision was to be the Number 1 salesperson overall. My short-term goal was to be awarded the salesperson of the month and securing the winner's parking bay for the next 30 days.

When I was becoming alcohol-free (AF), I had the long-term goal of being AF for 12 months. My short-term goal was being AF for that day or for a specific event or celebration.

Writing this book was a 12-month process and the short-term goal was just two chapters per month.

A compelling vision of the future needs to be more than "what you don't want": that's just survival.

As humans, we are motivated by both pain and pleasure. The downside of just using pain motivation, is that once you're out of the pain there is no compulsion to keep moving forward towards a bolder or brighter future.

Pleasure motivation keeps you moving towards your vision and goals. A vision that excites you, be it a cause, experience, physical thing, financial or health goal, if its meaning to you is strong enough, it creates the compulsion to keep you moving towards achieving it.

This is how we shift from survival mode to thrive mode.

A great place to start is to ask yourself this question:

What would I be doing if time and money were no issue?

Or if you won the lotto, what would you do? Or what causes touch you emotionally?

What or who are you grateful for that you would like to give back to?

Is there something new you have always wanted to learn, like a language or skill? What would you do once you learned it?

Find something that turns you on when you think about it. Now visualize yourself achieving it. How does it feel?

If you don't feel anything, dream bigger. The bigger the dream, the larger the desire, the greater the discipline.

If you're struggling with this, the perfect first step is to visualize something short term.

Maybe it's to go for your first walk in years, stop drinking alcohol for one day, take up yoga, write your first thank you card, make your first cold call, eat a healthy home-cooked meal, bank and save your first $10.

Remember: baby steps are one of the methods to change.

To reverse the rut, get your attention out of the past and into the present and towards a better future. We can build upon this first small step.

OK, once you have something in mind, write it down. What does your vision look like? It's essential to write it down so we can formulate the plan to make it happen.

Your Focused Game Plan

If all we do is imagine or dream about our compelling vision, then that's all it will be, *a dream*. This is why it's essential to write it down. From here, we can reverse engineer the process to achieve it.

The way we created our compelling vision, was to future pace and imagine a more desirable future.

Look at your written description of that better future and now let's reverse engineer the steps that it takes to go from that future reality, back to your current reality.

I am thinking back to my real estate business.

Our goal was to achieve $10 million by 2010 and to do this, we reversed engineered the steps to achieve this goal, based on an incremental increase of market share year by year in each of the suburbs we worked and served in.

Reverse engineering the process, and starting in 2010, we would have had 35% with 25 salespeople. In 2008/2009, we would have had 30% with 22 salespeople. In 2007/2008, 25% with 20 salespeople. In 2006/2007, 20% with 18 salespeople and so on, right back to the start date and current reality.

A weight loss or weight gain goal is precisely the same.

If you want to be 65kg in 6 months' time for your best friend's wedding and you're currently 6kg under or above your desired goal, your plan would be 1kg (up or down) per month for the next six months.

You could even write it using the "from X to Y by Z" formula. Let's say it's June and the wedding is in December. You would write your goal like this:

From 71kg to 65kg by December or from 59kg to 65kg by December.

What gets measured gets done and what doesn't get measured doesn't get done, so now we plan out the details.

With weight loss or weight gain, it's about measuring energy in and energy out.

In your Focused Game Plan, you'd plan your food intake, exercise, sleep pattern, and water intake each day and week to stay on track with your plan. You would set a desire or target for each metric and then record the actual result.

For my real estate business, we set targets and measured everything. The number of appointments, the number of conversations it took to get an appointment, how many houses we sold, how many properties were on the market, how many hours we trained each week, how many buyers we were taking through properties, where our advertising spend was going and more.

Any activity or action that you can control and schedule that effects the outcome you're chasing is called a "lead measure". The result is called the "lag measure".

It's best to be measuring both lead and lag; however, place most of your attention and energy on the lead measures, for these are the activities and actions you can influence. The outcomes will take care of themselves.

Now, back to your Compelling Vision and Focussed Game Plan.

I want you to reverse engineer the steps it would take to go from your desired future to your current reality. If it helps, break it down into quarterly, monthly, daily, or even hourly targets and steps.

What actions, behaviours or activities do you need to do to achieve these quarterly, monthly, daily or hourly targets?

If there are actions and activities within these lead measures that you need to repeat to achieve those lag measures, it's best to set up a routine to deliver your desired outcome.

This is what we call your Winning Routines.

Winning Routines

Just because you have a compelling vision or goal and a plan in theory to achieve it, doesn't mean it's a done deal.

Many people set goals, write them down and wonder why they don't achieve it.

Here's the thing. There's a saying that goes: "*We don't rise to the level of our goals. We fall to the level of effectiveness of our habits and routines.*"

We're creatures of habit. Over 90% of what we do is by habit or routine.

As we've discussed, we store repeated actions as habits in our subconscious, leaving maximum energy in our conscious mind for situational awareness.

Staying with the same ratio, it makes sense that those stored habits are what delivers over 90% of your outcomes.

If you upgrade or adjust your goals, target or vision, and they're different from your current reality, you need to improve or change your habits and routines.

In simple terms, if you want a different outcome, you need different routines and habits.

This means getting rid of old non-serving habits and routines. We will devote the entire next chapter to methods for breaking and changing old habits and how to replace them with new, upgraded ones.

For now, be mindful and reflect on some of your daily habits and routines, starting with how you rise in the morning.

Are you starting the day intentionally working on yourself? Or are you habitually checking your social media and email and reacting to other people?

How about the ritual of your commute to work?

Are you mindlessly listening to talkback radio and getting frustrated with peak hour traffic? Or are you using your time driving as your 'university on wheels', listening to educational or inspiring podcasts and audiobooks?

What's your mid-morning and lunchtime routines?

Are you buying whatever is convenient, habitually feeding your body the same empty, non-nourishing, high-calorie food? Or are you packing your lunch, feeding your body the nutrients it needs to perform at its peak?

Think about when you get home after a hard days' work. Is it your ritual to grab a beer or wine, lay back on the lounge and unwind? Or, do you get home, get changed in your activewear and go for a stress-relieving 30-minute walk or run?

Reflect on whether you have some habits and routines that aren't serving you anymore, especially with your new compelling vision and focused game plan.

Remember, we don't rise to the level of our goals. We fall to the effectiveness of our routine and habits.

Great. Now, you have the three pillars in place to create the best version of you.

Now it's time for the fourth pillar: Massive Action.

Massive Action

Peter Drucker once said:

Most people and businesses fail not because they lack strategy, but because they fail to *execute*.

A great plan that is never implemented will never beat a poor plan that is superbly executed.

Now don't let the title of this fourth pillar fool you.

Your first step in the direction of your newly created desired reality, even if it's a baby step, is Massive Action, even if it's in the opposite direction to your current lifestyle.

That first step, no matter how big or small, is the hardest one. You're bravely stepping outside of all that you know and becoming something different.

Every fibre of your body will be fighting you, trying to keep you safe in the security of the familiar, in the secure and loving arms of your known long-held habits and routines.

Your subconscious mind (actually your body as described by Dr. Joe Dispenza) is where all your habits are stored, and it will be screaming at you not to change.

Yet it's the compulsion of your Compelling Vision, the details of your Focused Game Plan and the promise of the power of your Winning Routines that will set you free.

These are what provide you with the courage to take the Massive Action you need to become the best version of you.

Every success I have experienced in my life or seen play out in the lives of my mentors and clients have all started with this critical first step.

As the famous Chinese proverb correctly states: "a journey of a thousand miles starts with the first step".

But you won't take that first step and each step after that to become the best version of you, unless you have the other pillars in full swing.

It's the vision of a healthier, wealthier, happier you, that will compel you to start eating better from your next meal and to save your first $10 next payday.

It's the vision of providing financial security for your family, that will inspire you to finish your MBA after hours and give up the weekend horse races with your mates to study.

It's the vision of becoming a soldier in the Australian Army, that will drive you to change every non-serving lifestyle habit and stop associating with the people who have been enabling you and holding you back.

It's the vision of becoming the Number 1 office in the country and all the people you get to help along the way, that gives you the commitment to believe in your plan, even when your friends and peers are laughing at you.

It's the vision to write a book and share your life and lessons that you know will help others, that fuels your courage to overcome your thoughts of not being smart enough to write your first paragraph.

Now it's your turn.

What's the first, right next step forward towards your Compelling Vision of the future, no matter how big, that represents Massive Action for you?

Remember, there is no wrong answer here. Only a courageous first step in the direction to becoming the best version of you. The person you were destined to become.

Finally, here's the reality of the situation. It's on *you*.

Repeat this affirmation: *"If it's going to be; it's up to me"*.

You are 100% in control of taking this Massive Action. You hold the power in the palm of your hand.

You have everything you need inside of you to decide to desire more for yourself.

You can back it up with the right thoughts, words and behaviours to bring it to life.

You weren't born to be average or to be in a rut. Life choices have got you to this current reality.

You were born to shine and more than once.

You have the opportunity to be the best version of you. Life choices can take you to this desired reality.

Right now, in this moment, you get to decide to believe either that your best days are behind you, or your best days are ahead of you.

It's your choice.

Make it.

CHAPTER 11: SETTING UP YOUR WINNING ROUTINES

On this fateful Thursday, I found myself sweating profusely in 40 plus degree heat in a completely foreign environment.

Not sure what was about to happen next, I could feel my heart rate rise rapidly. My breath was shallow and racing, heightening my senses. My body shifted into survival mode.

Around me, I could count approximately 15 other people I didn't recognise. Unlike me, they were calm, breathing normally, almost relaxed.

Trying my best to fly under the radar to blend in, I tried to hide my nerves and discomfort.

But it was apparent: I was the odd one out.

My 6-foot 3 inch, 115kg frame loomed above the smaller framed, lighter humans around me. Paranoia was setting in and I could begin to feel eyes settling upon me.

That's when someone with absolute authority stood in front of everyone. The people around me stood upright and stable, hands by their sides, eyes focused straight ahead without deviation. I followed their move, hoping not to bring attention to myself.

Without having time to react, it began.

On the outside, the sweat was pouring out of me.

On the inside, I was screaming for it to stop.

I was uncomfortable. My body was quivering. Seconds felt like minutes.

I felt physically, mentally and spiritually challenged in every possible way.

I wanted to give in, but I knew I had to hold it together and press on.

That's when the authority figure standing in front of us said:

"Change, release and breathe."

I had just held my first ever position at my maiden visit to a Bikram Yoga studio.

This was the first step out of my comfort zone and into the unknown.

I was taking small steps towards a brand-new habit that I wanted to create in my life.

Breaking non-serving habits and replacing them with serving routines, is key to reversing the rut and unleashing your full potential.

If you can master this, you can take back control of your life and your best days will indeed be ahead of you.

Keep in mind, your habits have taken months and even years to form. Changing them permanently is no overnight, quick fix. It's going to take time.

A study conducted by Professor Jane Wardle and Dr. Philippa Lally at the University College of London, revealed that it took 66 days for the research participants to create an automated new behaviour or habit.

In James Clear's groundbreaking book, *Atomic Habits*, he reports that *repetition* of a new desired habit is just as important as how long you do it for.

For example, if you practice your new exercise habit of walking for 30 minutes once or twice per week for 66 days, this would not be nearly as effective as, say, walking 4 to 5 times per week for the same period of total time.

It's a combination of committed repetitions and time, to break old habits and create new habits.

It may take you 30 days, three months or even a year to cement a new routine in your life. The point is to learn to enjoy the process of *becoming* and relishing the journey along the way.

With all of the above in mind, when it comes to breaking and creating new habits, be easy on yourself.

Habits are hard to break because they're well entrenched in your brain's neural pathways. If you fall off the wagon, jump back on and remember this is a marathon, not a sprint. Don't give up!

Remember, we are quite literally, "creatures of habit".

When we stop and think about the way we shower in the mornings, clean our teeth, put on our shoes and drive to work, we don't need to think about these activities. They are habitual.

This gives our brain space and energy to be on the lookout for new opportunities or unforeseen challenges to overcome.

It's a double edge sword, of course, because our brain doesn't know the difference between good and bad habits. It will merely create them after a series of repetitive behaviours.

So, we must sort out the non-serving, negative habits from the positive, life-changing ones that serve us in the best possible way.

To first change a habit, we need to understand the cause of it better.

You see, all habits are fuelled by a root cause or belief and have a reward for performing it. Some of these are functional, others not so much.

Here are examples:

- Habitually checking our email and social media several times per hour gives us a sense of connection, acceptance and belonging.
- Mindless eating is a form of comfort.
- Substance abuse like drugs and alcohol gives us some temporary escapism from the stresses of our life, just as unmonitored hours surfing the web creates a mind-numbing reprieve from boredom or tough times.
- Sticking one smoke in your mouth after another is a way of taking some time out.

Reflecting on some of your non-serving habits, are you starting to get some insights into the cause or the beliefs behind yours? When you do, you can begin to confront the real issues.

Let's look at some other examples from my life and my clients' lives.

You may have a belief that you need to drink to be social, attractive or loveable.

What if you learned to love who you are without having to be under the influence?

If your time on social media or gaming is a form of escapism or your way of avoiding fights with your partner, the real issue could be the pain of facing how dysfunctional your relationship has become.

Even if it makes you feel depressed, guilty or bad about yourself for having a bad habit, you're not likely to stop it unless you find another way to deal with its function.

You must put something positive in its place. Positive can also be painful but essential – like dealing with your feelings instead of stuffing them down with food or attending counselling with your partner instead of numbing your problems through mindless video games or excessive alcohol or drugs.

For me, I thought I deserved a beer after a hard day's work and had the belief that if I go to the gym before I cracked my first beer, it will counter-act any drinks I had that night.

The challenge was this: one beer always turned into two. Then a wine or two and then a whisky. This went on every night for several years. The rut of habitual drinking just got deeper the more I repeated it.

Now, let's get practical and start the process of reversing the rut of these non-serving habits. Thinking about what you have read so far, select a habit you want to break and replace.

Once you've identified the habit you want to change, bring what is usually unconscious (or subconscious) into your conscious awareness.

Now that you have it in your conscious mind, have a good look at what you're getting out of it.

In other words, what's the reward or function of it? How is this habit serving you? Are you looking for comfort in food? Numbness in wine? An outlet or connection online?

For me, that drink after work relaxed my mind and helped me to forget (literally) my challenges from the day.

Deep down, I knew this habit wasn't serving me and deep down, you know what's not working for you too. Trust and honour your wisdom, for it always knows when you're behaving in a way that doesn't help you live your best life.

Now use that wisdom to replace and build something into your life that will provide you with what you want.

Choose something to replace the unhealthy habit. What can you do instead that would serve you?

For me, I changed my coming home from work routine. Instead of going to the gym and getting pumped up and primed for my twilight beer, I swapped the gym for yoga, an exercise that challenged by body physically but also made me feel calm and relaxed in my mind.

I still got the reward of a calm mind without the need for alcohol. Knowing I needed to shed some body fat to better hold the postures and positions, I ate better and nourished my body.

OK, now it's time to introduce another weapon for your habit upgrades.

It's time to *harness the power of the pen*. There's something magical about committing a promise to paper. It makes that promise more real.

Write down your new habit or routine. Writing out a goal and keeping it handy to look at every day (or as many times a day as you need to), can help you stay on track.

This is why I love journaling so much. It's powerful! You can write the description of your new habit in your journal and read it as part of your morning routine. It's a soothing prescription that has no side effects and is likely to help you create great days ahead.

Finally, let's remove the triggers that activate your poor habit.

If Doritos are a trigger for your snacking at night, throw them out on a day you feel strong enough to do so. If you crave a cigarette when you drink socially, avoid social drinking for a while until you feel secure in your new habit.

One of the triggers for me was at the end of the day, driving home late in the afternoon. That's when I would get the "taste". My subconscious mind began to crave that ritual beer after work. I'd immediately feel the need to head to the gym, work out like crazy, then head to the liquor store to buy icy cold beers and a bottle of red for dinner.

The trigger point for me was the drive home, so I changed it from driving to the gym to driving to my yoga class instead.

Anything can be a trigger for your habits and routines, including people.

If you're trying to reduce your chronic alcohol consumption and you have a group of buddies that like to catch up for a drink, maybe it's time to spend less time with them until you have your alcohol-free habit in place.

On the positive side, people can help you with forming new habits and be great accountability buddies.

The same reason why you get better results at the gym with a personal trainer and the reason why many recovery programs include group meetings, individual sponsors or therapists, is that being accountable to others is a powerful incentive to keep on keeping on.

By giving and receiving support, you keep the goal in focus.

Working with a coach or mentor can help you deal with the basis of your bad habits and find positive, healthy ways to take care of yourself instead. Being accountable to a friend (in person or virtual) helps you stay on track.

I used five of my closest mates to support me on social occasions when I was breaking my regular drinking habit and going alcohol-free for 12 months.

Having as much support around you is critical to reversing the rut and unleashing the best version of you.

In my experience (and as a result of working with clients), routines and habits are hard to break because they are deeply ingrained neural pathways, which have taken months or years to form.

According to the neuroscientific theory called 'Hebbian theory', the more we repeat a task, the stronger our memory circuit becomes. In more simple terms, cells that fire together wire together. Therefore, through time and repetition of the new behaviour, we can reprogram our brain, forming new, automated responses or habits.

Be patient. It does take time.

We have to break the old, install the new and create new neural pathways. You can lay a solid foundation in a month, but it will take another 30 to 60 days to fully automate it. For some people, it may take a little longer, others less.

It all depends on the habit, your personality, your level of stress and the support systems you have in place.

Be gentle with yourself. You have to remind and reinforce that bundle of nerves in your brain to unwire, rewire and change from your default settings to your new desired way of being.

You must be mindful of your self-talk. Monitor your inner conversation and if it's becoming negative, stop it. Negative self-talk can seriously affect your ability to change and grow. That critical internal dialogue has likely contributed to your undesirable habits, so be kind to yourself.

If, when you catch yourself saying, "I'm fat" or "No one likes me" or "I'm not good enough", reframe it or redirect it. Reframing is like rewriting the script. Replace it with, "I'm getting healthier and healthier every day", or "My confidence is growing more and more each day".

Stop self-judging and don't believe everything you think, for not all thoughts are the truth.

This is why a mindset that believes **your best days are ahead of you**, backed up with a **vivid and compelling vision**, is so critical. It will pull you through the tough times if you stay committed to it.

Leverage your compelling vision by proactively visualizing yourself as the changed and desired version of yourself. Vivid visualisation helps to retrain your brain and keeps your self-talk positive.

One last tip: it's something I share in the Best Version of You Coaching Program.

Habit Stack. This means to use an existing serving habit that you want to keep and add a new habit or routine to it.

For example, if you want to introduce journaling into your morning routine and you always start your day with coffee.

As the kettle is boiling or the coffee is brewing, write in your journal. Once you've finished, as a reward, your beloved brew awaits as a delicious prize for completing the new routine.

Or let's say you want to write five thank you cards every day. Your regular finishing work routine is to shut down your computer and write your "to do" list for the next day, before tidying up your desk and leaving.

Wind up your day 5 or 10 minutes earlier and right after you write your "to do" list (before you tidy your desk), sit down and craft those five thank you cards as an addition to your current ritual.

The more you can add new habits to existing ones, the easier it will be wiring them to your neural pathways.

For me, adding yoga to my 'drive home' routine when the trigger of "the taste" kicked in, meant I rewired my circuits to crave the feel-good benefits of a great physical, mental and spiritual workout instead. Drinking booze only ever gave me a temporary fix with plenty of adverse side effects.

How can you habit stack right now?

As we wrap up this chapter, please be mindful that humans are not perfect and we may slip up occasionally. That's OK. If you fall, get back up. Almost everyone slips up. It's only human.

But it's not a reason to give up. It tells you what kinds of triggers push you off track. It tells you what you might need to change to stay on track. This is all part of your personal development journey and paying the price of learning.

Remember, there is no failure, only feedback, learning and then winning.

Take baby steps, if necessary. Even if you can't follow through 100% right away with a whole new habit, devote as much time as you can to your scheduled new practice.

For example, if you've blocked out an hour to exercise, but you have to attend an urgent, unscheduled meeting that only leaves you 30 mins to workout, do the short version that day. That way, you'll reinforce the message that "this is the time of day for my new habit".

Finally, don't be a hero. Get some support around you in the shape of supportive and positive people, create an environment that aligns with your desired new habits and always remember that time is your friend.

Your **winning routines** will help you become the best version of you. Step by step, you'll create a life that lights you up and allows you to reach your highest potential.

Your most significant victory is not failing or falling. Instead it's the courage you find to rise each time you stumble.

Chin up – your best days are ahead of you.

CHAPTER 12: GRATITUDE 2.0 AND MEDITATION

One of the most effective techniques you can use to reverse the rut and unleash your full potential, is to use the intentional power of **gratitude**.

The benefits of gratitude are widely accepted, but it's an excellent tool we often forget to access daily. It's almost impossible to feel both gratitude and any self-destructive emotional state of being at the same time.

From an energetic perspective, gratitude is a form of love.

Love is one of the closest vibrational energy states to a "life force", the quantum field or universal energy flowing through everything at the subatomic level.

This is where spiritual and scientific paths begin to merge.

The study of quantum physics has revealed, that the world and everything in it is made up of 1% matter and 99% energy and information.

The spiritual or religious world has a similar take on the concept of there being an energetic vibration around us.

For over 2000 years, Kabbalah has been speaking about the 1%

world and how 99% of us have a veil over our true purpose and world. Buddhism has a similar philosophy, that everything is energy.

Whether you're a believer or non-believer, atheist or religious, people around the world have used prayer and meditation for thousands of years to align, connect with and communicate with the natural energy of the universe.

Gratitude is one of the essential practices that helps us tap into this unlimited energy source in order to unleash our full potential.

In my view, there are two types of gratitude: Gratitude 1.0 and Gratitude 2.0.

Gratitude 1.0 is a feeling of thanks and love for something already achieved.

Gratitude 2.0 is when you feel thanks and love for something in your future you haven't yet achieved.

Remember: where your attention goes, energy flows. Our past is the sum of our known experiences. We create the future from the unknown.

Gratitude 1.0 keeps your focus and attention in the present and on the past.

Gratitude 2.0 redirects your focus and attention from the present to the future.

> **NOTE:** To download a visual of the "Gratitude 2.0 Model" and to leave a comment about your thoughts on the book so far, go to www.shanekempton.com/gratitude

Think about this from a practical perspective. All possibilities are found in the space or realm between our present moment and the future.

If we reverse engineer this thinking, there's only one path from our past to the present moment and that's the one that brought us here.

If we only stick with Gratitude 1.0, we focus on that one path from our past to the present. We play it over in our mind. We keep the same old habits on repeat, the ones that keep us stuck in the past or unable to envision the best days ahead of us. This makes each day (and our future) very predictable.

When we feel this kind of gratitude, our subconscious responds to the intention or energetic vibration of feeling love and thanks at that moment.

Gratitude 2.0 leverages this process and can 10x your progress by feeling gratitude for *future* possibilities.

When we focus our attention on our desired future reality, we move our attention away from the one path from our past and we open our energy to new and unknown options.

A quick side note here. Many people will try and change the results that are occurring in their lives. They will set New Year Resolutions, kickstart new business plans at the start of the financial year or upgrade their goals after seeing an inspiring motivational speaker.

This is a great start; however, unless they upgrade the routines that deliver the results, nothing will change in the long term.

For example, $100,000 per year routines won't deliver a $250,000 result simply because you wrote it down.

You won't lose weight if your current routines are stacking on the kilos.

Something has to *change*. Remember, we don't rise to the level of our goals. We fall to the level of the effectiveness of our routines.

Our current set of routines and habits are driven and determined by who we are as a person, that is, how we show up each day.

Willpower might change your routines in the short term, but we often run out of energy and revert to the habits of our current or past self in no time.

To experience long term and constant upgrades to your routines, you need to work at the cause level, that is, *who you are being as a person*.

When we upgrade who we are being (and becoming), we feel a shift and upgrade in our behaviours and routines. Ultimately, this upgrade will cascade into our overall results.

In my experience, the most effective way to upgrade who you are being as a person is an 'inside out' job. You have to do the inner work and a great place to start is the future.

As a result of continually feeling grateful for our desired future and aligning our intention to this reality, we begin to 'Be' this new version of ourselves.

It's almost like we're time travelling, remembering our future like we would remember our past. Instead of remembering the good old days of our past, we live the good new days of our future.

Gratitude 2.0 is the ultimate feeling of receiving.

Now don't get me wrong: Gratitude 1.0 (being grateful for what you have already created) is healthy, especially when its coupled with Gratitude 2.0.

If you are happy with your life, be grateful. If you're not satisfied with where you're at, find things to be happy about right now and be thankful for what you want to achieve in the future.

Remember, it's a balance of being both humble and hungry, ambitious and appreciative.

Too often, we wait for something external to help us upgrade our lives, when what we need is an *internal shift*.

If we rely on something external to fill a void inside of ourselves, we instantly set ourselves up to fail.

Life doesn't give us what we want or need. It gives us what we deserve from who we are Being. This is an internal state. We must Become that upgraded version of ourselves to feel the emotional state of that person.

In more simple terms, life is not HAVE DO BE, it's BE DO HAVE.

NOTE: To download a visual of the "HAVE DO BE Model" and to leave a comment about your thoughts on the book so far, go to www.shanekempton.com/be

That is, once I HAVE the Mercedes Benz, then I'll DO the phone calls to prospects and then I'll BE that successful person.

Or once I HAVE the ripped body, then I'll DO the gym work and then I'll BE that pro athlete.

Or once I HAVE a fantastic relationship with my partner, then I'll DO the loving things and then I'll BE that amazing partner.

The correct formula is BE DO HAVE.

That is, BE that successful person, then you can DO the phone calls to prospects and then you'll HAVE the Mercedes Benz.

BE that pro athlete and then you'll DO the gym work and HAVE the ripped body.

BE that amazing partner and then you'll DO the loving things and HAVE a fantastic relationship with your partner.

The starting point for this whole process is **Gratitude 2.0**.

When you live your life in this state, you'll be grateful for things you haven't even achieved yet. You'll start to feel like the shiny, bright, upgraded version of yourself from that desired future reality.

The more often you hold your attention there, the more often your energy flows towards this intention. You start to BE and maintain the state of mind of this new person, leaving the non-serving version of yourself behind.

So how do we hold this intention of Being the upgraded version of ourselves more often, so we can initiate the BE DO HAVE process?

We use the **power of meditation**.

Now when some of us hear the word meditation, we picture images of Zen-like yogis sitting cross-legged in the middle of a rainforest, or Buddhist monks chanting in long orange robes.

The reality is: you can do meditation anywhere. The technique is simple and doesn't take years to master or special equipment or training. Anyone can do it and you can start today.

There are some excellent books dedicated to this process, two of which I highly recommend grabbing a copy of:

- "*Breaking the Habit of Being You*" by Dr. Joe Dispenza
- "*Innercise*" by John Assaraf

I see meditation as simply a mental rehearsal of your desired future self.

It's Gratitude 2.0 and the 'BE DO HAVE' process in motion. You rewire your brain, from always referencing that one path from your past and connecting it to all the possibilities of the future.

SO, let's walk through how it works.

Bring your state of being into the present moment.

From the present moment looking forward into the future, there are unlimited options, exciting opportunities, endless possibilities.

Getting into the present moment can be difficult because our daily environment is filled with seductive distractions.

Pick a time of day and location when you know there will be less distraction.

Make sure you quieten your five bodily senses and disconnect, so you can connect with the infinite possibilities of the unknown.

I like to meditate early in the morning as part of my morning routine.

There is a beautiful window of time in my life between 5:00am and 6:00am when no one else is up in my house, the traffic is light, and the distractions are low. My mind is still relaxed from the night's sleep and so my mind chatter is minimal. You might find your magical window at some other time – do what works for you.

The books I mentioned above explore some great science, which points to the fact that first thing in the morning and last thing at night are the best times to get into a meditative state. It's when your mind and body are naturally best prepared and in an optimal state to meditate.

So, where is the best spot to meditate? I deliberately get out of bed to meditate, as I want to condition my mind that bed is for sleep and nothing else.

I don't sit crossed legged or kneel 'samurai-style'. I sit on a chair in a quiet part of the house, with my eyes closed, back straight, earplugs in and my hands are resting comfortably on my lap.

I then use the breathing technique I mentioned earlier in the book to calm my mind and prepare it for meditation.

Breathing in through my nose for a count of 5 and then exhaling through my mouth, like I'm blowing through a straw for a count of 8 to 10. I do this cycle five to ten times or as long as it takes to feel calm and in the present moment.

Once my mind is quiet, I focus only on the vastness of space and time.

Like in the movie *The Matrix*, when Neo plugs into the construct program, all I see and feel is nothing. No past. No future. Just the endless now.

It is at that exact point where we unlearn everything from our past and we begin to relearn what it takes to achieve our desired future.

At this point, my brain circuits are quiet. I begin to visualize my compelling vision and future life with precision, emotion and clarity. I see and feel everything from that desired future reality.

I'm experiencing it in my mind as I've already achieved it. I'm virtually 'future pacing' my life and emotionally connecting to that incredible future.

Now I can feel warm gratitude for this inspired future reality and for the person I have become to achieve it.

OK. Stay with me here team – this is deep and vitally important to understanding why this process works.

As mentioned earlier, most scientists and spiritual teachers agree that we are 99% energy (including everything around us) and 1% matter, existing in a realm often referred to as the 'quantum field'. The frequency of energetic vibrations creates what we perceive as form or matter.

The vibrational frequency of Gratitude 2.0, that is, when we're feeling deep emotions towards our compelling vision for the future, is our optimal creative vibrational state. It's closely aligned with the vibrational frequency of the quantum field.

It makes sense, then, that when we're aligned with the creative energy of all things, all things are possible. In Kabbalah studies, it's called the 'equivalence of form'.

What this means is that when we feel deep gratitude, we feel the energetic vibration of love. Love is aligned to that 'quantum field' of energy.

It's where all possibilities exist. It's also where we can discover our future, 'upgraded' selves.

I find that the longer I stay in this state of gratitude and love, the higher the impact of my meditation.

Eventually, when I want to come back to the present moment, I set the intention, open up my eyes and stand up. I physically step into the shoes of the upgraded version of myself and choose to BE this person.

I usually meditate for 15 to 30 minutes, but I don't set myself any specific time frame. Instead, I allow the process to unfold naturally.

From there, I grab my journal and write down some thoughts, intentions or goals that have flowed from that meditation to reinforce the process.

This also helps to unwire the circuits of the 'old you' and begins to rewire new circuits to create the 'new you'.

Do this daily and before long, you're constantly BE-ing and DO-ing and feeling and experiencing life as your upgraded self. The HAVE-ing will then naturally take care of itself.

The tip here is to be proactive with your thoughts.

You can do this anywhere! In the morning or at night. When you're stuck in traffic, going for a run or a walk, or when you're sitting at the doctor's surgery waiting for your appointment.

You can do it anytime your thoughts usually run aimlessly or drift back to the past. You can choose to meditate upon your desired future reality wherever you are.

If you recall my story when I was training to get into the SASR, my mind was always focused on that desired reality.

The personal affirmation I repeated over and over expressed gratitude for achieving that lofty goal. My compelling vision was an obsessive thought and I gave my passionate attention to it daily.

In closing, you have to want that desired future reality more than your current zone.

Whatever it is you want to achieve in the future, it has to be an obsession, to the point where you focus all of your conscious attention on it whenever you have the time to do so.

You live it, breathe it, eat it, smell it, taste it.

You experience the emotions of achieving it whenever it's in your conscious mind, well before it ever becomes a reality.

My Gratitude 2.0 Meditation is a fantastic, proactive way to start or end each day. You can bookend your mind with love for a compelling future. You can't but help to think and feel: "*My best days are ahead of me*".

Now that you're beginning to master your mind, fend off negative thoughts, resist the seduction of the 'good old days' and ignore the doubting self-talk, you have the skills and knowledge to step up and out of that rut.

You can leap forward and blaze a new trail of infinite possibilities.

Don't accept the default option.

It's time to unleash the best version of you and live a life by design.

It's time to stop wasting energy being a Worrier. It's time to BE a **Warrior**.

CHAPTER 13: BECOMING THE ROUTINE WARRIOR

People rarely fail in strategy – they fail in implementation. In simple terms, they fail to follow through and apply what they've learned or mapped out.

Success is all in the execution. That's why the fourth pillar of the Best Version of You Blueprint is "Massive Action".

In this chapter, it's time to bring all the theories, techniques and practices you have learned in this book and implement them into your life, using the power of proven systems and routines.

It's time to become a Routine Warrior.

There is a fine line between a rut and a routine. The biggest difference is that a rut is a reactive habit and a routine is a proactive behaviour.

What we need to do is build positive momentum, by taking baby steps towards your best days and creating daily routines that reinforce the upgraded version of you.

The best place to start is at the beginning, that is, at the start of your day. Let's create a powerful morning routine. As the poet

Rumi once said: "The morning breeze whispers wisdom, so don't go back to sleep".

There are several amazing books written on the power of a morning routine; however, my two standout favourites are "*The 5am Club*" by Robin Sharma and "*The Miracle Morning*" by Hal Elrod.

Both speak of the inspiration found at this special time of the day. It's a magical, serene time where you get to be you, before the rest of the world awakens.

I have experienced the wonder of an early morning ritual and so have many of my clients. For me, it includes meditation, exercise and journaling, ticking all the boxes from my mind, body and soul trinity.

An **empowering morning routine** is how we reverse the rut and set the tone to be the best version of ourselves each day. I want you to take pride in your morning starts and your training routine. I want you to enjoy it, love it and own it!

The 60 Minute Morning Routine

Make the most of your mornings by trying this 60-minute health hack (ideally at 5:00am).

Get centred: 10 to 20 minutes

Disconnect from distractions and connect to whatever it is that you feel drawn to. Whether it is to the beauty of nature, the strength of God or to your 'source'. Pray or meditate by walking through nature or sitting still, as I do, wherever you are.

Exercise: 20 to 30 minutes

Move your body every morning. Do some yoga, go for a cardio-busting run, walk the dog at the park, pump weights at the gym, hop on your bike – anything that gets your heart rate up (to a safe level for your age and fitness level) for a sustained period of time. Resistance training is also vital for mature men and women.

Journal: 5 to 10 minutes

Write in your journal. I use these four headings: "Yesterday's Wins", "Today I'm grateful for", "My intention for today is" and "My goals for today are".

If that's too much, write down some thoughts from your meditation or set your goals for the day. Write down three things you want to get done so you can make those a priority before the busyness of the day takes over.

Daily Warrior Routines

Becoming a Routine Warrior is about having the Winning Routines, systems and habits to support your Compelling Vision.

Let's explore what I've used to support the Master Life Model and BVOY Blueprint that effectively manage my time, routines and personal priorities.

Self and Time Management

It's my passionate belief that by being more controlled and disciplined in your life, you gain more freedom. These success systems genuinely represent who I am, what I stand for and are the backbone and cornerstone of being a Routine Warrior.

The best first step in this process is to keep a "time log".

Similar to a food diary, this is where you keep a log or diary of where you spent every 15 to 30mins throughout the day for a one or two-week period.

Once you have created the record, review it to see where your time is going.

Examine each task and ask yourself:

- *Is this task appropriate for me?*
- *Could I use technology to assist me with this task?*
- *Is there a better time to do this task?*
- *Could I delegate this task?*
- *Is this task essential?*

Once you have reviewed your time log and have created a list of tasks, you can delegate. You can either delegate them to an existing team member, technology, or turn that list into a job description and potentially hire someone or virtual assistant to do them for you.

Ok, now that you know where you're spending your time, use this list of techniques below to become even more efficient as you transform into a "Routine Warrior".

Using Transport to Transform and Transition

Personal and professional development is a *must* when it comes to reversing the rut.

Learning new things and being inspired by positive true stories and the latest research keeps your mind stimulated and firing on all cylinders. It illuminates and ignites your passion for being the best person you can be.

Finding or making time to do this consistently is critical. Habit stacking and leveraging other routines is an effective way to do this.

Try using your commute to and from work (or your trip to and from a regular destination or even time spent doing household chores), as a state management routine.

I use the drive to work to transition from father/husband to coach/speaker. During this time and throughout the day, I'll listen to inspirational audiobooks to supercharge my personal development and ingest information in small but meaningful bursts.

I use the drive home to transition from coach/speaker to father/husband, by listening to fun music on the radio and chillout tunes to unwind.

Block Out Time

Often, we're good at keeping appointments with clients but not as great at keeping them with ourselves.

By blocking out time in your diary for your own appointments, you increase the odds that you won't schedule someone else's priority into your schedule.

It guarantees 'me time'. Block out time in your diary for appointments with your clients, yourself and your loved ones – don't just use it as a way to diarise your professional commitments.

Make sure you include exercise, dinner dates, play dates, meditation/prayer, eating times, travel times, everything and anything that requires your time and commitment and is important to you.

Master your time

By now, you're starting to know what's important to you. It's time to apply some daily disciplines, to ensure you are completing (Doing) the necessary tasks to fulfil your commitments to yourself, as you become the best version of you.

These are my most potent routines for staying on track with the Master Life Model, BVOY Blueprint and your Compelling Vision.

There are many definitions of success and failure. Jim Rohn captured it beautifully when he said:

"Success is a set of small, daily habits repeated over a period of time. Failure is a set of small, daily habits repeated over a period of time."

If something needs repeating, it needs a system or routine. We have to know whether what we're repeating is keeping us "on track" or "off track" on our journey to becoming the best version of ourselves.

The skill is knowing the right habits. You can identify these once you know what is important to you.

We call them **Your Big Rocks**.

Your Big Rocks are the mission critical, non-negotiable routines and habits required to be the best version of you for your family, friends, career, friendship, health, wealth and community.

So how do we begin? Here's where to start:

Create an Ideal Day

Create your perfect day and build in all of the key tasks required to achieve your life goals.

By scheduling and proactively performing these key tasks and routines, we maximise our chances of success.

If we repeat our ideal day for 5, 6, or 7 days, we end up with an ideal week.

If we keep repeating our ideal week for 4 to 5 weeks, we have an ideal month.

If we do this for 12 months, we have an ideal year.

As you can see, it all starts with what we have scheduled for *today*.

Master the 6:2:8

My favourite way to create an ideal day, is to pick 6 to 8 things you can do between the hours of 6:00am and 8:00pm, that will have the biggest impact on your plan and give you the most significant returns on your time and energy investment.

Those 6 to 8 things are tied directly to tasks or habits, repeated daily over time, to ensure success and help you nail your life goals.

For example, health and personal growth are important to me. That's why I invest 60 minutes every morning to exercise, meditation and journaling to stay on top of my game.

As a young real estate sales rep and later the CEO of an international brand, and now, as a global speaker and coach, no matter how busy I am each day, I've always given my morning routine absolute priority.

I've worked on my spirit through meditation, my mind through journaling and my body through exercise.

Family is another one of my Big Rocks. Every day, I tell my wife and children that I love them and have at least one sit-down meal with them (depending on who's home at the time).

In my selling days, sending out five hand-written thank-you cards daily was one of the 6 to 8 daily disciplines I used to help my business grow.

The critical point here is to define your Big Rocks clearly and know the action steps required to achieve them. Break these down into smaller daily routines and over time, they will help you produce amazing results.

A quick tip:

Experience has shown me that more than eight routines is overwhelming. Less is always more, so you might find yourself with 5 or 6 key daily routines that are more effective and have a greater impact on your day and your life. It takes more discipline, personal leadership and focus to say no to less important things in your life. Practice the art of saying 'no' if you feel things are beginning to overwhelm you.

Self-Mastery

It is up to us to control our time, our desires and our passions. By choosing to be a Routine Warrior, we become the true masters of ourselves.

No amount of money or fame can buy your ability to command your daily routines. It's an ongoing journey of self-mastery and a constant test of our character.

It requires resolve and intestinal fortitude, especially when we're at our lowest or when temptation is high. It requires even more resolve when we've reached the mountaintop and all of life's temporary feel-good experiences are at our fingertips, whether they're good for us or not.

Most importantly, self-mastery is about *balance*. Put family and fitness priorities in place that are non-negotiable. Take control of your time and your energy. Carve out time with your loved ones.

The key to a balanced life is ensuring you devote adequate and quality time to the mind, body and spirit, as outlined in my Success Trinity. Our Mind-Body-Spirit connection is where our strength, will, determination and hope originate from and where true fulfilment lies.

Once we've mastered ourselves, we can begin to express our full potential and the best way to do this is in service to others and the world.

Expressing Your Full Potential

This is a privileged life. Now it's time to live it.

For me, there is no greater privilege than to live a life where you express the full potential of your unique talents in the service of others. This is the shared purpose of the human species.

The world needs a diverse range of skills to solve the many challenges we face. This is why unleashing the full potential of the Best Version of You into the world is critical.

This is the journey of self-mastery. It's about shining our authentic light on the world and helping others to do the same. It's where we seek holy moments of selfless service and the opportunity to apply our gifts to make the lives of those around us better.

It requires moment by moment awareness, discipline, routines, habits and mindfulness in the pursuit of better days ahead.

In the words of Jim Rohn, the prize is well worth the price. Self-mastery and discipline are a far easier price to pay compared to the deep regret and unfulfilled potential of staying in a rut.

Objectives and Virtues of a Routine Warrior

To ensure success without the side effects, you also need to embrace these five non-negotiable objectives and virtues that give meaning to your habits and life.

Spirituality – Purposefulness:

When you're centred and connected to your source of inspiration, you get a sense of clarity and purpose. Maintain a cheerful, willing, can-do attitude and focus on goals that are helpful to the greater community.

Relationships – Gracefulness:
Be inclusive and respectful. Recognize the diversity, worth and dignity of every single person and express genuine concern about their well-being.

Health – Discernment:
Have the courage to determine what's right and what's wrong and then take action to support your health goals. Controlling our desires and wants, whether in solitude or amongst friends, gives us strength and a sense of self-respect and makes our life goals much more achievable.

Intellectual – Humility:
Be grateful for what you have, for what you've achieved and for what you are going to achieve. Be humble and willing to learn, seek advice and allow others to have opinions, preferences and ideas that are different from yours without compromising your own beliefs.

Financial – Intestinal Fortitude:
Have the resolve to follow through on your commitments, objectives and duties and be committed to the details. Always be mindful and accept the consequences of your words and actions.

Living the life of a Routine Warrior requires an investment of your time, energy, focus and efforts. If you neglect any of these five objectives and virtues, you may achieve success; however, you will also likely experience adverse side effects.

For example, financial success through neglect of your relationships results in a lonely victory.

Relentless intellectual studies with a diet of McDonalds and Coke and little or no exercise can result in a shortened life span or reduced quality of life.

Obsessive fitness routines that sacrifice your productive business time can result in unreliable service or poor job security.

Or success in all areas of your life, but ignoring your spirituality, can result in an unexplainable empty feeling that cannot be satisfied by any worldly matter.

Live the life of the Routine Warrior and you will not only feel a sense of fulfilment and harmony in your own life, but you'll also see a positive ripple effect on the lives of others.

CHAPTER 14: YOUR BEST DAYS ARE AHEAD OF YOU

"Life can only be understood backwards; but it must be lived forwards."
Soren Kierkegard

I want you to trust that your best days are ahead of you.

To do this, you need to trust that you can live your best life, starting from where you're at right now.

It doesn't matter if you've made mistakes or indulged in bad habits or let yourself or others down. You can start from this present moment and choose your best life.

Let's summarise what I've shared with you throughout this book, starting with the five elements of the Master Life Model.

The Master Life Model
Causality
Reversing the rut starts with your world view.

Holding the intention that your best days are ahead of you (and not behind you) is the key to opening the wondrous doors of possibility that lie ahead.

By understanding there is a cause for every effect and that there's no such thing as 'suddenly', we proactively choose to live our lives at the cause level. We take responsibility for actions and consequences.

This gives you back control of the 'controllable', namely yourself.

You become the cause of your own life, the master of your fate, the captain of your soul.

Belief

Believing in something bigger than yourself gives you purpose, which is a strong motivator. Purpose gives you a reason to press on when things feel tough. It brings meaning to the hard work that you put in.

You may believe in a worthy cause, a movement, in mastering your career, in building a business, contributing towards a charity. It's any belief or mission that helps you make a positive difference, gives you the chance to serve others and contributes to genuine and lasting change.

Having belief in something bigger than ourselves gives us one of the most potent remedies to reversing the rut and seek out those best days to come. It's called 'hope'.

Seek out something you are passionate about and embrace it fully.

Attention

Where our attention goes, our energy flows.

By having something bigger than ourselves that drives us and gives us purpose, we begin to focus on something other than ourselves and create a bright and positive future.

This is how we shift from "past-present" thinking. We divert our attention from the one path that got us here and move it to a "present-future" focus.

This opens up vast and infinite possibilities. Instead of spiralling downwards, we begin to reverse the 'doom' loop and we can clamber out of the rut towards those better days.

Focus your attention on contributing to a better future and your life will improve dramatically.

Significance

With our attention, energy and efforts channelled on a cause that is bigger than ourselves, we now need to turn inwards and work on ourselves.

To contribute to a worthy cause and improve things outside of ourselves, we must educate ourselves along the way.

To grow and to become better is a natural human desire. How will you serve the world? What do they need that you and your talent can provide?

This is all about finding *significance*. Share your time, your talents, your treasures.

We cannot measure in dollars the time we spend with a sick friend, or playing with our daughter, or supporting a colleague, or serving those in need in our community. It is priceless.

Living a life of significance, is about the positive feedback loop of continually working on yourself and serving others at the same time.

Continue to grow and learn so you can continue to add value and serve.

Belonging

We humans are pack animals. We are better together.

When we proactively 'cause' our life, believe in something

bigger than ourselves, continue to improve and serve others, we naturally want to share this with other people who believe in what we believe.

Seek out a group of people you can grow and learn with, share and laugh with – a community of like-minded individuals who have your back.

Collaborate with people who hold a genuine desire to support each other through the highs and lows of life. The ones who hold you to account and help you chase your dreams and are there to weather the inevitable storms.

Join a tribe of people who believe in what you believe and believe in *you*.

The five elements of the Master Life Model is what we use to reverse the rut and work towards a future filled with the best days you can imagine.

Now that we have a solid foundation to build upon, it's time to unleash your full potential in life. We do this by following my Best Version Of You Blueprint.

The BVOY Blueprint

Compelling Vision

Write down your compelling vision for the future with crystal-clear clarity.

Picture it in your mind – visualise what your life looks like. What do you look like and what are you doing?

Who are you hanging out with? Describe it in vivid detail, the smells, the sounds, the emotions you feel when you're living life in this desired future reality.

It's about getting clarity about what you truly want. Remember: where our attention goes, our energy flows.

Focused Game Plan

As the saying goes, a goal without a plan is just a wish. A compelling vision without a plan is just a dream.

You have to want to win and plan to win.

Map out everything you want in detail and have a game plan for all areas of your life: wealth, relationships, partner, family, career, social, community and any other area of life that's important to you and forms part of your compelling vision.

Be flexible as things change and always be prepared to adapt if you need to.

Winning Routines

As I've said before in this book, we don't rise to the levels of our goals; we fall to the effectiveness of our routines and habits.

We are creatures of habit and we form these consciously or unconsciously.

Remember: if a behaviour, action or task needs repeating in your life to achieve your compelling vision, proactively create a routine for it.

Be mindful of any unconscious habits and routines you have in your life that may not be serving you and replace them with life-affirming, healthy habits that bring out the best version of you.

Massive Action

Finally, most people, businesses, or organisations don't fail in strategy and planning.

It's the execution and implementation that lets them down.

Think big, start small, act now is a great way to get started.

Don't wait for everything to be perfect. As entrepreneur and life coach, Marie Forleo often says, clarity comes from engagement, not thought.

Let action create the clarity for you. You may have to feel the fear and start anyway. Ask yourself this: what is the first, right next step for you after reading this book?

Conclusion

I'm honoured and humbled you proactively chose my book as one of your growth experiences.

Writing it has been a labour of love. The process of sharing my experiences and what I've learned along the way, has cemented and clarified my mission to be the best version of myself and inspire others to do the same.

Together, we can have a positive impact on the world, be it with your immediate family, clients, work colleagues, community or the planet.

To do that, I'm building a global army to join me in this quest.

My sincere hope for you, is that this book is one of many more pilgrimages of growth in your life, a stepping stone in pursuit of your best life.

If you would like to continue your learning journey with me, I'd love you to check out my **Best Version of You Bootcamp Coaching Program,** an online coaching program designed to help you create and implement the BVOY Blueprint and live your best life.

I also love speaking, whether it's to an office of 5 people, a workshop of 50, a function of 500 or a conference of 5000. My keynote talks are high energy, entertaining, educational and super practical, with easy to implement and ready to use skills and resources.

To book me for a keynote or to find out more details, head over to my website at www.shanekempton.com

If you believe in what I believe, have enjoyed reading this book and you want to have a positive impact on the world too, I'd also be honoured if you referred it to a friend, family member or colleague.

If you've found yourself in a rut, please know that you are not alone and you can get yourself out of it.

If you feel you are in one now, please apply what I have shared with you in this book. Know that the models and techniques have worked for my clients and me, and I know they will help you reverse the rut and start living your best life.

If you're struggling with life right now, it's a strength and not a weakness to ask for help, be it from a friend, family member or professional. Put your hand up and ask. The first step is always the hardest, but rest assured it is worth it.

I believe in you. Why?

Because I know everyone can be the best version of themselves. It is inside of you.

You might find it hard to summon up those internal resources, skills and beliefs that have been dampened by years of challenges, setbacks and life scars, but it's never too late to start and it's always worth it.

Right now, it may feel a long way away. But this journey of 1000 miles is worth taking. It's worth taking that first step.

The world needs your special gifts and talents. You have a unique story. Your rut, your struggles and the story of how you overcame them could be the very thing someone else needs to hear about. They don't need to define you, but you may be able to use them to serve others and create your best life.

Who would of thought the son of a single parent who grew up in a small country town in Western Australia, left school after high school, had no university qualification to speak of, was bankrupt at age 24 and joined the army to get his financial life together, could make it in business and find so much success and happiness in his life.

If you're reading this book, it means you have the gift of sight and the ability to learn. All you have to do next is implement. Apply. Take that first step, no matter how small.

Remember to download all the models and resources referenced in this book, by visiting my website www.shanekempton.com/resources. While you are there, please leave a comment about what you thought about the book and what was most valuable to you.

I look forward to seeing and hearing about the unique gifts and value you bring to the world as you unleash your full potential.

Here's to you becoming the best version of you.

Your best days are ahead of you.

Shane Kempton

So, what's next?

I believe both mine and your best days are ahead of us.

Using the wisdom of all my experiences, I want to have an impact on the lives of those who are stuck in a rut or feel helpless and lost, living in the good old days of their memories.

In the years leading up to me writing this book, there's been an increase and much needed focus on men's mental health.

Over time, I have become a mentor for men looking for more meaning and fulfilment in life, and my journey into this world started with the motorcycle club that we set up for our modern-day veterans.

As you read this, I am proud to say that the club is continuing to grow and provides ongoing support to those brave men and women who chose to wear the uniform and now need our help.

For too long, men have been conditioned to "harden up" and get on with the job. We learn to suppress our deepest feeling and emotions.

Except we know through medical and scientific evidence that being in a state of 'dis'ease for prolonged periods results in disease.

Unless men have a group of tight, like-minded friends who they can be vulnerable with and share their highs and lows, they tend to bottle things up and push it deep down below.

They are afraid of seeming weak or not manly enough. Some may "hit the bottle" to numb the pain and to escape briefly from the burdens they carry.

Men often shelter what's troubling them from their spouse or partner to seem secure, dependable and reliable. Hiding our feelings for too long can then end up bringing us to our knees, weakened by the load we've been carrying on our own.

As a man who's seen the highest of highs and the lowest of lows, I'm privileged to have a tight group of good mates I can call on and a family that loves and supports me, especially when I've been on my knees.

I'm now in the perfect place to give back and support other men looking to reverse the rut, helping them trust that their best days are ahead of them.

I am 100% certain that part of the solution is getting back to the fundamentals of community and genuine connection.

If you go back just a few centuries, you'll find many men used to gather together regularly. They would sit around a fire and be social, tell stories, laugh and share their life experiences, often over a feed and mug of beer or wine.

In our modern '24/7' world where instant gratification is the overwhelming theme, hyper-connectivity can hinder our ability to connect with our communities in a significant way. Our smartphones in our pockets, our eyes on bright screens, swiping up and down, left and right.

Many men don't catch up like they used to and they get stuck in the rut of work, stress, eat, escape, sleep, repeat.

On the odd occasions when we gather together, the ladies chat in the kitchen and the men hover around the TV to watch sport, checking the scores of other matches and events on their phones. Women naturally share and talk openly, while men try to be "good at being a man", by hiding any weaknesses and masking their vulnerability.

I'm on a mission to break this cycle and lose the stigma of being a man who can open up and share his feelings with others.

I want to shift the social conditioning that leads to men thinking they have to "man up". I want it to be a sign of strength that you put your hand up and say, 'Mate, I need your help'.

The start of this journey is getting around a group of like-minded, big-hearted men, who believe in the same cause or have the same values and support this new definition of being a man.

Let's use what we know worked for thousands of years. Let's go back to a time when men shared stories and food, laughed and solved problems over a brightly lit campfire.

I've turned this ancient ritual into my modern-day version called the "Steak Sandwich Men's Get Together" (**SSMGT**).

It's designed to get those men who may find themselves in a rut, stuck on the lounge at home every night, mindlessly watching TV, who may feel lonely and isolated, as they have no supporting friendship network. These men could be family men or single, getting in a rut doesn't discriminate.

The "Steak Sandwich Men's Get Together" (SSMGT) was formed to provide an opportunity for these men to get up off the lounge, out of the house and to meet with other men, to laugh, to share stories with and to do life together one steak sandwich at a time.

Every couple of weeks, we choose a pub that has a legendary steak sandwich. It's a casual, social environment with no pressure or agenda. Just blokes getting together to chat with like-minded and light-hearted blokes.

This is not about a long night on the grog or partying on into the early hours. Typically, each get together goes for a couple of hours at the most and we start early (around 6:00 pm), so it doesn't carve out too much time away from loved ones.

It's just long enough to have a bite to eat, a drink if you choose and the opportunity to chat about life or simply listen and feel like you are part of a supportive group.

It's not a piss up and we all need to drive, so no one goes too hard on the beers. It's about being social and having an enjoyable experience: banter and some laughs are a must.

Importantly, we hold each other to account.

Each group sets the culture and the ground rules, such as no phones, because we're here to talk. No judgment or belittling, because we're here to support each other.

It's not therapy, so if someone needs medical or professional assistance, we refer them to the right kind of service so they can get help.

Above all, it's about new experiences, so we go to a different venue every time.

We focus on the present and the future and offering up solutions, with the firm belief that our best days are ahead of us. Sometimes, one person will buy dinner for another brother who can't afford to pay for dinner that week, so there's a real sense that we've got each other's backs.

As I write this chapter, the SSMGT is building momentum.

It's capturing the attention of men looking for something to belong to and experts in the field who love what we've created. We've even had local businesses wanting to get behind the movement through sponsorship.

My vision is to see a "Steak Sandwich Men's Get Together" happening every week, in every city or town, all around Australia and then the world. A place where men can come together socially in a safe, healthy environment to talk and 'do life' together.

From here, men can begin to reverse the rut, look to better days ahead and become the best version of themselves.

On the near horizon, my vision is to take a group of men from SSMGT to walk the Kokoda Trail in New Guinea.

It's an historic place in Australian Military history and holds a special place in my heart and the hearts of many other Australians.

The Kokoda Track is just under 100km (60 miles) overland through the Owen Stanley Range in Papua New Guinea and is a pilgrimage for many Aussies.

This is where our parents, grandparents and great grandparents fought to defend Australia against invasion in World War 2. It is a physically, mentally and emotionally challenging, but ultimately, rewarding 10-day adventure hike.

I want to use this hike as a way to help men to reverse the rut and to begin their journey of becoming the best version of themselves.

Using the Master Life Model, committing to walking the Kokoda Track will give these men a sense of purpose and something to believe in. It will require them to focus their attention on the task. Also, they will gain significance and self-worth as they improve their physical and mental states along the way.

They will be doing it with other like-minded and light-hearted men, so they will feel a sense of belonging.

Finally, they are at 'cause' level, making the decision to commit and proactively choosing to feed their mind and bodies in positive ways as they prepare for the gruelling trip.

It's a compelling vision for me and I'm experiencing Gratitude 2.0 right now as I think about it. I can already feel the emotions of what it will be like for that group of fathers, sons, brothers, grandfathers, uncles and mates after pushing themselves and each other for ten days to complete such a goal.

If you'd like to know more or get involved, please touch base via my website www.shanekempton.com

I am committed to helping you become the best version of yourself, just as I continue to grow and learn and strive to do the same.

I can say with absolute clarity and confidence: our best days are ahead of us.

Shane Kempton

About Shane Kempton

6 foot, 3 inches tall and 110kg, Shane Kempton is born, bred and proudly Western Australian. He has experienced life and business from many perspectives and at the highest level.

From serving his country as a soldier working alongside the Australian SASR, business owner of Australian's Number 1 real estate office (Harcourts and Roy Weston Group) and CEO of three national real estate groups to Founder and President of a Military Motorcycle Club which looks after our veterans to hosting Sir Richard Branson for Breakfast and raising in excess of $160,000 for charity, Shane has lived life to the full.

Shane's three-decade obsession with self-development (which continues to this day) has created a very unique blend of life experiences:

- Small business and corporate success
- Time in the military, working alongside Special Forces Soldiers
- Membership in some of the world's most secretive societies
- Playing and coaching elite sports teams
- Hanging out in the dark world of motorcycle gangs

- Studying many of the world's religions and walking the path of mystical spiritual ways
- Charity work including assisting our modern-day military veterans, and
- Promoting good men's mental health.

His life's journey, with all its ups and downs, successes and failures has placed him in a very unique situation. It's gifted him with the foresight and ability to dissect the above experiences and find the golden thread of success that weaves itself around all of them.

Using his down-to-earth and approachable style, Shane shares his unique and powerful insights, to a variety of industries, through his inspiring and entertaining conference keynotes and through his easy to implement coaching and mentoring methods.

Happily married with four adult children and three grand-children (who affectionately call him Grand-Dude), Shane continues to learn, grow and share, knowing both his and your "best days are ahead of you".

Stay in touch.

w. Shanekempton.com
fb. ShaneKemptonCoaching